ALSO BY THE FIRESIGN THEATRE

The Complete Plays of The Firesign Theatre

"Anythynge You Want To"
"Marching To Shibboleth"
"Profiles in Barbeque Sauce"

By Taylor Jessen and The Firesign Theatre
"Duke of Madness Motors"
The Complete "Dear Friends" Radio Era
"Box of Danger"
The Complete Nick Danger Casebook

By Peter Bergman
with David Ossman and Phil Fountain
"Trolling The Woe"

By David Ossman
"Dr. Firesign's Follies"
"The Ronald Reagan Murder Case"

EXORCISM IN YOUR DAILY LIFE

The Psychedelic Firesign Theatre
At The Magic Mushroom — 1967

The Complete Plays of
The Firesign Theatre,
Volume 3
4 or 5 Crazee Books
2012

EXORCISM IN YOUR DAILY LIFE
The Psychedelic Firesign Theatre
At The Magic Mushroom — 1967

BY PHILIP AUSTIN, PETER BERGMAN,
DAVID OSSMAN AND PHILIP PROCTOR

Published in the USA by:
BEARMANOR MEDIA
P.O. BOX 71426
ALBANY, GEORGIA 31708
www.BearManorMedia.com

Credits & Thanks:

Most photographs by John Rose
"Bridey Murphy" October 1967 poster by Anton Greene
Nat Freedland column from the Los Angeles Free Press,
November 3, 1967

Rights to perform these Firesign Theatre radio and stage plays are available from the Authors. Please query Comedic Rights at www.firesigntheatre.com. Rights to perform "Waiting For The Electrician," "Nick Danger," "Don't Crush That Dwarf" and "Temporarily Humboldt County" in versions adapted for the stage are available from www.broadwayplaypubl.com.

The Firesign Theatre's website is **firesigntheatre.com**

ISBN-10: 1-59393-214-6 (alk. paper)
ISBN-13: 978-1-59393-214-5 (alk. paper)

Printed in the United States of America.

Cover design by Phil Fountain, Oz Design Group.
Edited by David Ossman and Taylor Jessen
Designed by Valerie Thompson.

First Edition.

THIS ONE IS FOR

THE WIZARD OF RADIO FREE OZ

Our Marx Brother

Peter Bergman

Contents

EXORCISM IN YOUR DAILY LIFE

The Psychedelic Firesign Theatre At The Magic Mushroom — 1967

THE MAGIC 'SHROOMS

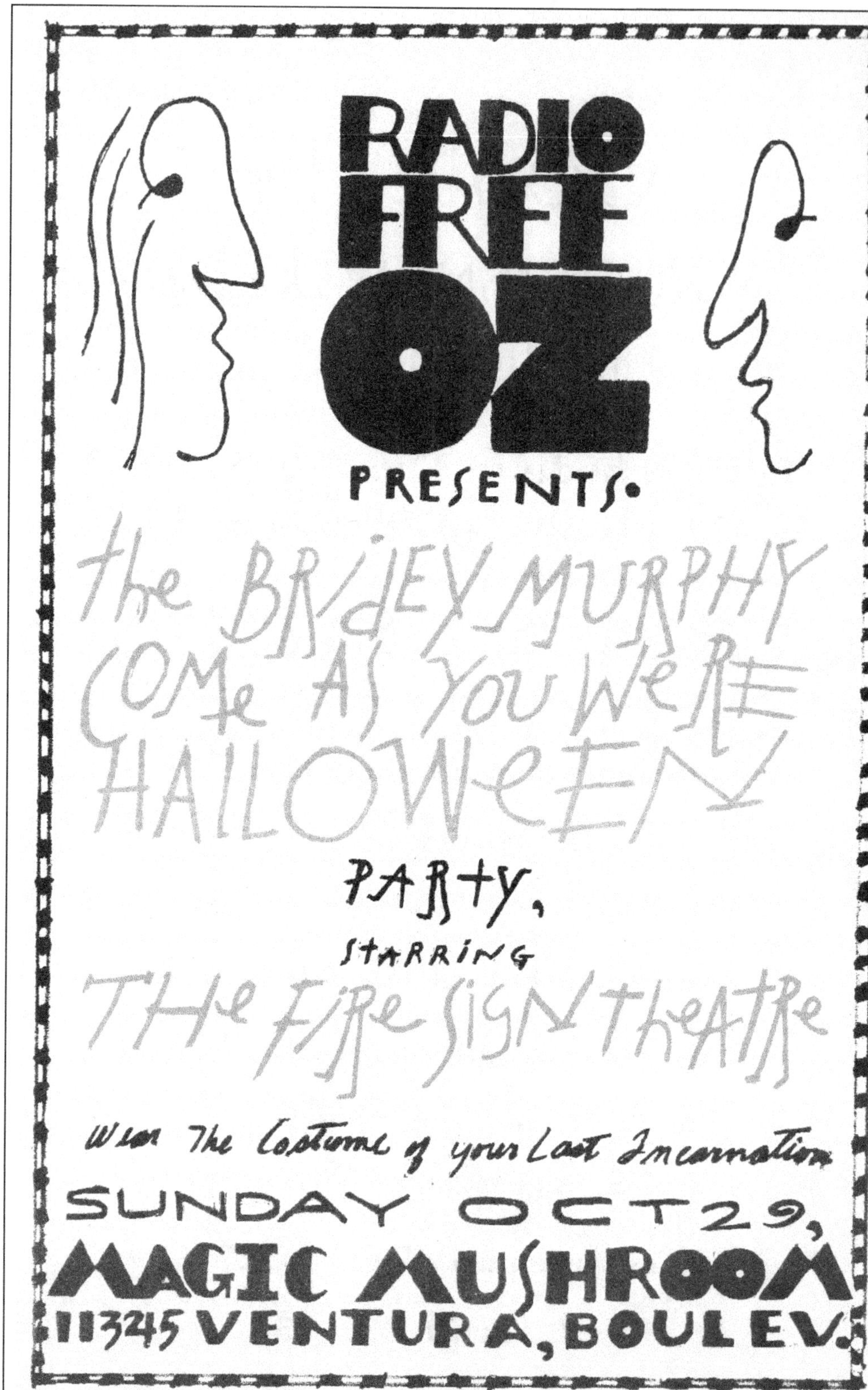
RADIO FREE OZ
PRESENTS.
the BRIDEY MURPHY COME AS YOU WERE HALLOWEEN
PARTY,
STARRING
THE FIRESIGN THEATRE
Wear The Costume of your Last Incarnation
SUNDAY OCT 29,
MAGIC MUSHROOM
11345 VENTURA, BOULEV.

Wailing

by Nat Freedland
Los Angeles Free Press, Nov. 3, 1967

Meanwhile, back at Avant-AM, Sunday night has been turned into a sort of Intellectual Ghetto by KRLA. The first hour of Radio Free Oz has been chopped off for John Carpenter documentaries and a rather cryogenic Derek Taylor segment.

Dave Ossman's groovy chick, Tanya the bodypainter, was rounding up press reviewers for the First Annual Bridey Murphy Come-As-You-Were Halloween Party at the Magic Mushroom with Peter and the Bergmen. The featured attraction was supposed to be the World Premiere of Columbia comedy album "Waiting For the Electrician or Somebody Like That."

But for reasons never explained, the album wasn't premiered and the entire three hours of Radio Free Oz was devoted to new live shticks by the Firesigners — which was a mistake.

Wizard Peter's truest bag is Occult Sincerity, not Occult Humor. The most memorably eerie moments of both the KPFK and KRLA incarnations of Radio Free Oz came when Bergman hypnotized the audience into thinking each night's enthusiasm was somehow the Great Symbolic Answer To It All. Whether Peter's guest is an acupuncturist or an astral spirit, the old Wizard somehow convinces you every time.

But even for sorcerers, three solid hours of hip humor is a bit much to attempt. It's not surprising that the Halloween Free Oz was pretty skimpy at the final weigh-in. The surprise was that about one hour of Theater Oz was toplevel sidesplitting fun.

Despite Peter's current star trip and sideline hypes, Ozland has managed to retain its magic through every change. Even on a red-lit little stage, without incense, in a prettydelic but sprawling rock-club, the otherworldly feeling comes through.

The Magic Mushroom was only about a quarter-filled when the show went on the air at nine, but Peter kept zinging out the address every five minutes when he got on the air like it was another KPFK marathon. He must have honed in on every car-radio dial-twirler along Ventura Blvd., because the Mushroom was jammed by 10:30.

The high point of the Halloween show was a brilliant skit about "Exorcism and Your Daily Life" as produced by the Urpy Educational Film Co. The structure of the sketch is far too freaky to be explained in short order, just let it be said that every familiar cliché you never thought about was trotted out through a looking glass.

The only other worthwhile items on the Ozgenda were the solo contributions of Phil Proctor, who is now a bulwark of the Mark Taper Forum Repertory Company. Phil led into the final raga with the best Ralph Williams take-off ever. The showroom location kept changing from Eczema to Noxema and other fine South Cal. Towns. He was equally gutbusting as Pastor Flash of the Electrical Torch Church and in the first few Dr. Astro horoscopes. (Your sign is Gregarious, your birthstone is reinforced concrete.) Phil even saved the seemingly endless Flying Saucer Nut Convention skit with his dual portrayals of a drunken "mental photographer" and rotten H. Bill William Archer of Proof Magazine. At one point Proctor did a tour-de-force argument between his two voices in the sketch. He was a gas.

EXORCISM AND YOUR DAILY LIFE
and
THE SEANCE

Written by The Firesign Theatre
Performed live at the Magic Mushroom and broadcast on KRLA-AM on October 29, 1967.

ORIGINAL CAST — EXORCISM
Phil Austin as Bob, Dr. Filth
Peter Bergman as Mayor Simmons
David Ossman as Announcer, Dad, Miss Cratch
Phil Proctor as Jimmy, Ollie

ORIGINAL CAST — SÉANCE
Phil Austin as Doc Beeson
Peter Bergman as Martha Washington, Manager Mouse, Andrew Johnson
David Ossman as George Washington, Teddy Roosevelt
Phil Proctor as Astral Operator

Exorcism and Your Daily Life

NOTE:	*Poor quality film sound at top and end made with finger vibrating lips.*
VOICE 1:	Eleven — ten — nine — seven — five — three —
VOICE 2:	Sound
VOICE 1:	One
VOICE 3:	Start
MUSIC CUE:	*TITLE THEME*
ANNOUNCER:	URPI Classroom films presents Educational Film B-151, "Exorcism and Your Daily Life."
MUSIC:	*UP AND OUT*
JIM:	Gee, Dad! What a bummer!
DAD:	Why, what's the matter, Jimmy?
JIM:	My Civics teacher assigned me this dumb paper on Exorcism, and I'm supposed to go play ringball with Bruce. I mean, what does Exorcism have to do with me, and ringball, and Bruce?
DAD:	More than you can ever imagine. I used to feel the same way you do about exorcism, Billy. But your mom and I learned long before you were born the real importance that it has in all our lives.

JIM: But, I don't even understand what it means, Dad.

DAD: Ha, ha. Well, in a manner of speaking, Willy, "exorcism" is a transitive verb meaning to expel an evil spirit from or out of a person or place by invocation or use of holy names. It's akin to the Greek "herkos", a fence, with its cognate "horkos", an oath. Whence, "hokizein", to bind with an oath. Thence "exocizare". That's Low Latin.

JIM: Gee, Dad, I still don't understand.

DAD: Well, Timmy, let's go see my old friend Bob Brown at the bank.

JIM: Again?

MUSIC: *HARMONICA FALL*

SOUND: *KNOCKS AND DOOR OPEN*

DAD: Good morning, Bob.

BOB: Morning, Bob. Morning, Tommy.

JIM: Hi, Mr. Brown.

BOB: How have you been since you were here this morning, asking about capillary action?

JIM: Fine, Mr. Brown.

BOB: Good. Well, what is it now? "Wheat Production in the Great Northwest"?

JIM: No.

BOB: "The Gross National Product of Sweden"?

JIM: Golly, that's close.

BOB: "Our Animal Friends"?

JIM: Cold...

BOB:	Exorcism?
JIM:	Yes! I have to write this dumb paper...
BOB:	Now, hold on son. You wouldn't call it "dumb" if you knew about exorcism what my old friend Mayor Simmons knows. Why not go and see him...?
MUSIC:	*HARMONICA FALL*
SOUND:	*KNOCKS AND DOOR OPEN*
DAD:	Good morning, Mayor Simmons.
MAYOR:	Morning, Bob. Morning, Freddie. Well, what is it this time? The Australian Ballot? Representative Government in Postwar Indochina? The Cultivation of Sea Kelp? Our Internal Waterways?
JIM:	No, Exorcism, Mr. Mayor.
MAYOR:	Now, Billy, I can tell you this — if it weren't for exorcism, Merleyville wouldn't be the town it is today. Take a look at this graph...
JIM:	That's very interesting, Mr. Mayor, but I already know about the pancreas.
MAYOR:	Then take a look at this other graph...
DAD:	It's shaped like a pie.
MAYOR:	Have a piece, Sammy. Now, that piece of pie is equal to the 14 percent of the Merleyville town budget that goes for exorcism. Sounds like a lot, doesn't it?
DAD:	Sure does. I've been meaning to talk to you...
MAYOR:	It may sound like a lot now, but — remember the trouble we had when I first proposed it at the town meeting...
CROWD:	*MUMBLE, BOO, IMPEACH MAYOR SIMMONS*

SOUND:	*GAVEL RAPPING*
MAYOR:	Citizens of Merleyville!
MISS C:	Mr. Mayor!
MAYOR:	Yes, Miss Cratch?
MISS C:	How can you expect the citizens of Merleyville — already bled white by your corrupt machine — to spend another 14 percent of our pie on Exorcism — whatever that is...
MAYOR:	Miss Cratch, as our Civics teacher, you of all people should realize the importance of exorcism in this efficient and democratic working model township.
OLLIE:	That's all very well, but aren't we here to talk about the Corn Smut that's ruining our crops?
CROWD:	MUMBLE MUMBLE — CORN SMUT — RAZZ
MAYOR:	Exactly, Ollie! Take a look at this working model...
MISS C:	But we already know about the Refining of Petroleum Byproducts!
MAYOR:	Ssshhh! Exactly, Miss Cratch. Let me turn the working model on.
SOUND:	*CLICK — THEN VARIOUS MACHINE SOUNDS UNDER*
MAYOR:	Now, as you can see, these little red trucks here, with the two-and-a-half men on the side, drive up with their 118 percent of 1964 capacity oil loads and deposit them in those five-and-a-half black buckets, which are then lifted to the 75 percent over parity mark through these little broken lines, ending finally in John's Gas Station as fuel for our cars and farm machinery, at the Lignite Mine as kerosene to light the lamps of the workers, to Mr. Foster's Cola factory as artificial

coloring, and the rest is exported abroad by Mr. Artunian to make nylon stockings...

OLLIE: Then, there's none left for insecticide!

MAYOR: Exactly, Ollie.

OLLIE: And that's why we got a corn-smut epidemic!

CROWD: *IMPEACH HIM, BOO, LACKWIT, BOSS SIMMONS, SSSSS, EXORCISE HIM! RAZZ*

CROSSFADING TO:

MUSIC: *HARMONICA FALL*

MAYOR: ...And that's how it all happened, Frankie.

JIM: Gee, Mr. Mayor, I sure see how exorcism ties into oil refining, but I still don't think I have enough for my dumb Civics paper. I mean, how does it all fit into Our American Way of Life?

DAD: What Ronnie means, Mayor, is how does it all fit into Our American Way of Life?

MAYOR: I might be able to fill you in on that — I've got a working model working over here someplace... But, actually, you'd probably do better to talk to my friend Bob Brown, down at the bank...

JIM: Again?

DAD: Well, actually, Mayor Tweed, we just came from Bob's office...

MAYOR: Oh. Well, let's see who else is open at this time of night... You might try kindly old Dr. Filith, down at the Armenian Medical Association...

MUSIC: *HARMONICA FALL*

SOUND: *KNOCKS AND DOOR OPENS*

DOC: Now just soak it twelve times a day and keep off your side as much as possible. I'll give you a subscription for petroleum jelly... Oh, hello, Kenny and your Dad. What's troubling you — you don't look at all well. Want an upper?

DAD: No, Doc, my teeth are fine. It's Lennie, here. He's got to write a dumb Civics paper on exorcism, and Mayor Simmons suggested we visit you...

DOC: Fine! Just take off your shirt and sit over there. I'll turn the lights out and (CLICK)... Now, this first slide is the gestation of the frog...

JIM: Geeeee!

DAD: No, Doc. What Mickey wants to learn about this week...

DOC: (CLICK) This is one of the many great Impressionist cathedrals...

JIM: Woweee!

DAD: No, no, Doc! Exorcism...

DOC: Oh! Why didn't you say so? Let me just set up this audiovisual projector... Here we go...

SOUND: *RUNNING FILM PROJECTOR*

VOICE 1: Eleven — ten — nine — seven — five — three

VOICE 2: Sound

VOICE 1: One

VOICE 3: Start

MUSIC CUE: *TITLE THEME*

ANN: URPI Classroom films presents Educational Film B-152, "Ringball and Your Daily Life."

MUSIC: *OUT*

JIM: Dad! What a bummer!

DAD: Why, what's the matter, Jimmy?

JIM: My Civics teacher assigned me this dumb paper on Ringball, and I'm supposed to go exorcise a dybbuk with Bruce. I mean, what does ringball have to do with me, and exorcism, and Bruce?

DAD: More than you can ever imagine. I used to feel the same way you do about ringball, Harold, but...

HIS VOICE FADES AWAY WITH THE MUSIC

The Séance

PETER: In the true spirit of Halloween we have with us this evening Doc Beeson...

Doc Beeson, a character from Firesign's "W. C. Fields Forever" sketch is a metaphysician and spiritualist, given the challenge of raising the dead. His first attempt is less than Top 40.

THE RAISING OF THE FIRST SPECTRE

PETER: Why that's Phil Spectre.

DAVID: But *he's* not dead.

PROCTOR: He hasn't had a hit in a long time. (RAZZ)

PETER: We'd like to speak with the greatest President of the United States.

DOC: I'm going up now. First bardo, second bardo, mezzanine, third bardo...here we are. All right you spirits, settle down... We would like to communicate with the greatest President of the United States...of America...quiet! Such a holocaust and clamor! I can't hear a thing. I'm afraid it just can't be done. I'm just not hot tonight.

DAVID: Isn't there some other method?

DOC: Yes, there is one, but it'll take a lot of time — if the audience won't get too restless I'll give it a try. Ooooooo Ooooooo Oooooooperator...

ASTRAL OPERATOR: Your call please.

DOC: Okay — who do you want?

DAVID: We want to talk with George Washington, the father of our country. Surely he must have some words of wisdom for our troubled times.

DOC: Operator? Do you have an astral listing for a George Washington?

OPERATOR: What location?

DOC: Mount Vernon, fifth bardo.

OPERATOR: One moment please.

SOUND: RING — RING — CLICK

MARTHA: Hello?

DOC: Hello, is George Washington available for plasmic manifestation?

MARTHA: I'll have to see. He's in the shower. (CALLS OUT) George?

GEORGE: (OFF) What is it, Marthie?

MARTHA: There's a medium on the phone.

GEORGE: (OFF) Take a message.

MARTHA: They want you to do your plasmic inevitable.

GEORGE: (OFF) I'll be right there.

DOC: He'll be appearing soon, right about over there...

GHOSTLY SOUNDS — AUDIENCE GASP

PROCTOR: He hasn't got any pants on!

DAVID: Shh!

GEORGE: My fellow colonials, the Revolutionary War was the least I could do for every American boy between the ages of 17 and 76... (FADES OUT)

PETER: That was amazing! (AD LIB) Are you strong enough to try it again?

DOC: (COUGHS) Sure. Who is it this time?

DAVID: Let's try Teddy Roosevelt. The Father of Our Foreign Policy.

DOC: Oooooooperator.

OPERATOR: Your call, please.

DOC: I would like to speak to a Theodore Roosevelt.

OPERATOR: What city please?

DOC: San Juan, Puerto Rico.

OPERATOR: Do you know the area code, please?

DOC: Second bardo.

SOUND: TELEPHONE RINGING

MANAGER: Astral-Famous. Manager Mouse here.

DOC: Can I please communicate with Theodore Roosevelt?

MANAGER: This is his manager, who wants to talk to him?

DOC: There's a group of people on the mortal plane here...

MANAGER: Where's here?

DOC: Los Angeles.

MANAGER: Is this one of those Ouija board calls?

DOC: No. This is in regard to a plasmic manifestation.

MANAGER: Hey Teddy, legit gig on the phone.

TEDDY: (OFF) Bully.

MANAGER: Here he is.

TEDDY: (OFF) Charge!

OPERATOR: Is this a charge call?

DOC: I'll get it, operator. I've got my Diviners Club Card.

OPERATOR: Thank you. Go ahead.

DOC: Okay, here he comes...

GHOSTLY SOUNDS — AUDIENCE GASP

PROCTOR: President Roosevelt, do you have any message for us here on Earth?

TEDDY: Walk softly and carry a big schtick. (MOVES OFF) Charge!

PETER: Wait, Mr. President; isn't there anything else?

TEDDY: My fellow Rough Riders, the war with Spain is the least I could do for every American boy between the ages of 18 and 98.

PROCTOR: Have we lost him, Mr. Wizard?

PETER: Yes, Jimmy.

PROCTOR: Golly!

DOC: Who's next, boys? I'm getting tired. The medium needs a massage.

PETER: I personally have a lot I'd like to ask President Johnson.

	He's so hard to reach these days. Do you think you can get to him?
ALL:	(AD LIB) *He's* not dead, is he? I don't know, ask Doc Beeson. Well, he's in a trance.
DOC:	(SINGING) I could have tranced all night, I could have... Ooooooperator...
OPERATOR:	Your call please.
DOC:	Do you have a listing for a President Johnson please?
OPERATOR:	One moment please... I have no listing for an astral form with that name, but there is a listing in the lowest bardo. Just outside of Naples.
DOC:	Put us through.
OPERATOR:	That area code is 666.
DOC:	Thanks, operator.
OPERATOR:	You're welcome...
SOUND:	RING RING — ASSORTED SCREAMS AND MOANS
JOHNSON:	My fellow souls-in-torment — quiet, quiet, please you all, I'm on the Hotline —
SOUND:	MOANS
JOHNSON:	Cool it —
SOUND:	MORE MOANS
JOHNSON:	*Aw, hell!*
SOUND:	SCREAMS
DOC:	Is this the disembodied soul of President Johnson?

JOHNSON:	Let me look — yep. Who's this call coming from?
DOC:	The mortal plane — Earth.
JOHNSON:	Oh, really? How's my body doin'?
DOC:	It's President of the United States...
JOHNSON:	Still? Well, I'll be damned —
SOUND:	SCREAMS
JOHNSON:	Come to think of it, I am. What kind of a job's it doin'?
DOC:	It's got us into a bloody conflagration.
JOHNSON:	Oh yeah. I know all about that. Intervening in that war between the people of the South and the people of the North was the least I could do for every American boy between the ages of 19 and 84 —
SOUND:	SCREAMS
JOHNSON:	Now hold on there! It weren't no worse than any other war. Just men shootin' and cannons boomin'...
DOC:	And napalm —
JOHNSON:	Na — Palm? What's that?
DOC:	Jellied gasoline dropped from jets onto Vietnamese villages. Sticks to the skin and burns people to death.
JOHNSON:	OOOH AAAH!!! That's horrible!
SOUND:	SCREAMS
JOHNSON:	I don't understand. What's this Jets? What are Viet-Namese?
DOC:	Wait a minute. Is this the soul of Lyndon Johnson?

JOHNSON: Why hell no! This is ANDREW Johnson!

SCREAMS SEGUE TO RECORD, "I PUT A SPELL ON YOU."

KALEIDOSCOPE
LIGHT SHOW
MACRO-BIOTIC DRINKS
11345 VENTURA BLVD
STUDIO CITY
877-9971
SUNDAY JAM SESSION
2 30 TO 8 00 PM
LIVE RADIO FREE OZ
8 30

THE LAST TUNNEL TO FRESNO (Doesn't Stop Here Anymore)

Written by The Firesign Theatre
Performed live at the Magic Mushroom and on KRLA-FM on November 5, 1967.

ORIGINAL CAST

Phil Austin as Artunian, Rafferty, Hayakawa, Marquis de Sade

Peter Bergman as Von Mist, Colonel Merkin

David Ossman as Kommendant Gruber, Field Martial Law

Phil Proctor as Dai Llewellyn, Delessups, Herbst, Ashberry

THE LAST TUNNEL TO FRESNO (Doesn't Stop Here Anymore)

OSSMAN: Ladies and gentlemen, Open City presents The Firesign Theatre in THE CONRAD AIKEN DILLEMMA...

AUSTIN: The scene — occupied Armenia, 1942...

OSSMAN: Three...

AUSTIN: Three — bitter cold winds whipping across the frozen tundra as a thin sun rises over Maximum Security Compound 13.

SOUND: DISTANT DRUM ROLLS

KOMMENDANT GRUBER: Ames?

BERGMAN: Here.

KOMM: Gridley?

AUSTIN: Here.

KOMM: Vigoda?

PROCTOR: Here.

KOMM: Leary?

BERGMAN: Here, there, everywhere.

KOMM: Freedland?

AUSTIN: Here.

KOMM: Vespucci?

PROCTOR: Here.

KOMM: Kosciuszco?

BERGMAN: Here.

KOMM: Larson?

AUSTIN: Here.

KOMM: Hayakawa?

PROCTOR: Hi ya, Kommendant.

KOMM: Quiet. Gurdjiev?

BERGMAN: Here — here — here.

KOMM: Kitchener?

AUSTIN: Here! Here!

KOMM: O'Brien?

PROCTOR: Here.

KOMM: Cohan?

BERGMAN: (SINGS) "Over There!"

KOMM: Usher?

AUSTIN: Fore!

KOMM: Krishna?

PROCTOR: Hare, hare.

KOMM: Remus?

BERGMAN:	Here.
KOMM:	Jones? Jones? Blind Little Willie Abraham Lincoln George Washington Diana Ross Watermelon and the Supremes Jones?
PROCTOR:	Who's playing Jones today?
AUSTIN:	I'll take it. Here!
KOMM:	Why are you always so late, Jones?
AUSTIN:	(LIKE STEPEN FETCHIT) I's jest so shifless... (AD LIBS)
KOMM:	Quiet! Van den Miewe?
BERGMAN:	Here.
KOMM:	Psacoropolis?
PROCTOR:	Here.
KOMM:	Artunian?
ARTUNIAN:	Morning, sir.
KOMM:	Henderson?
VON MIST:	Ja vohl, mein Kommendant!
KOMM:	Just a minute. Who is that man? Three steps forward!
VON MIST:	Eins, zwei, drei, "here!" Gut morgen, mein Uberkommendant!
KOMM:	Are you sure you're Henderson? You don't look a thing like you. This man is a fraud!
VON MIST:	Psst! Kommendant, don't you recognize me? I'm Von Mist, the camp undercover informer.

KOMM:	Oh, yes. Very clever disguise, Von Mist. All right! Back into ranks — Henderson — hee, hee.
VON MIST:	Dankeshoen, mein Kommendant. Drei, zwei, eins, there!
PROCTOR:	That was close, Henderson.
VON MIST:	Sure was, thanks, guys.
KOMM:	Brady?
AUSTIN:	Here.
KOMM:	Oswald?
PROCTOR:	Here.
KOMM:	Finnegan? Finnegan?
BERGMAN:	(WHISPERS) Wake him up.
AUSTIN:	Hereagain.
KOMM:	Llewellyn?
DAI:	(SINGS) When you tunnel in the ground...
KOMM:	Where is that voice coming from?
AUSTIN:	(GERMAN) Right under your feet, Kommendant.
DAI:	...and you're breaking out in song...
KOMM:	Breaking out in song again, are you Llewellyn? Well, I'm glad to see you're happy.
AUSTIN:	(GERMAN) All prisoners present and accounted for, Kommendant!
KOMM:	Good. Now, men, since you are all going to be here for the duration, there are a few things we have to get straight. I am very pleased with your behavior the last

few days, so the movies are on again. Tonight — The Cabinet of Dr. Caligari.

MEN: no no moan

KOMM: Quiet! You want another Andy Warhol festival?

MEN: I like Caligari! I can dig it! Ja vohl.

KOMM: All right, then! Point zwei. Yesterday, the officer's mess sank into the ground. I suspect the possibility of a tunnel.

MEN: What?

DAI: (SINGING AS ALWAYS) When you tunnel —

BERGMAN: Shut up, Llewellyn. (SOCK)

KOMM: Let me reiterate. Escape is impossible. This is not the first time rumors have come into my ears concerning an escape plot. Is there perhaps any truth to these rumors?

VON MIST: Ja vohl, mein Kommendant!

KOMM: Shut up, Henderson!

MEN: Good work, Henderson... Atta baby...

VON MIST: Thanks, guys.

KOMM: There has never been an escape from the compound, and there never will be an escape from this compound, or my name isn't Kommendant Gruber. That is all. I'm leaving now.

HERBST: Oh no you're not, Kommendant Gruber, because you're not Kommendant Gruber. Let me see your nose.

SOUND: MASK PULLED

MEN: Why, it's Henderson...!

HERBST: And this should prove to you men that such tricks as this will not go undiscovered, or my name is not Uberkommendant Herbst. I'm leaving now.

RAFFERTY: Oh no you're not, Uberkommendant Herbst, because you're not Uberkommendant Herbst. Let me see your beard.

HERBST: Ow!

RAFFERTY: Oh, yes, you are Uberkommendant Herbst. And I'm in trouble.

HERBST: No you're not — you're Gunther Arrest. Take him away. No, not that one!

MEN: Nice try Henderson...

VON MIST: Thanks, guys.

HERBST: I'm leaving now, but I'll be back soon for inspection. Be ready.

MEN: He's gone...what do we do now...

FIELD MARSHAL LAW: All right, chaps. Gather round. We've got a lot to discuss and get done if we're going to be out of here by tonight as planned. Now, Dai, give your report on the water damage to tunnel B...

DAI: When there's water in the mine, then the miner's going to die.

MEN: Shh, Llewellyn...

ARTUNIAN: Excuse me, sir, but I've got a fix on the Kommendant through the window, here.

LAW: Good lad.

MEN: Way to go, kid. Atta boy.

ARTUNIAN: He's entering the northwest corner of the compound. 1000-1, 1000-2, he's out of sight of the sentry tower,

1000-3, 1000-4, he's making a sharp 90 degree turn, 1000-5, walking up the 36 degree rocky incline on a direct azimuth with his office. 1000-6, he's in.

LAW: Well, Artunian?

ARTUNIAN: ...uhhh...pi R squared and take six from 34, carry the two... Sir, the distance between here and the water tower has changed again. It's 42 yards this time, and the last 12 yards are out of the line of sight of the blockhouse.

LAW: Splendid, Artunian. And how does this fit into our escape plan?

ARTUNIAN: Well, it doesn't exactly fit, sir, but don't you think it's interesting? I figured it out without any instruments...

VON MIST: Wunderbar, Artunian.

ARTUNIAN: Gee, thanks, Henderson.

LAW: Now then, we're all agreed. The escape will take place at midnight tonight through Tunnel R. Captain Delessups, our Chief Engineer, will give us the final plan of maneuvers.

DELESSUPS: Did you say Tunnel R, sir?

LAW: Of course, Delessups.

DELESSUPS: Well, we could use Tunnel R, sir — for a while. But we filled up the last half of it with dirt from Tunnel C. So we'll have to take a detour through Tunnel N.

LAW: Well, that's all right...

DELESSUPS: No, it's not, sir. You see, Tunnel N doesn't go anywhere.

LAW: It doesn't?

DELESSUPS: Well, it does and it doesn't, sir. It does go all the way through to Tunnel O, but it's monsoon season in Tunnel O. So my suggestion is that we use Tunnel D.

LAW: Well, jolly fine...

DELESSUPS: Not exactly, sir. We did get rid of most of the marsh gas in Tunnel D but it does run pretty close to Tunnel P, which the Germans are using for training.

MEN: What a bummer...

DAI: Oh no matter what you say, I'll go home in Tunnel A...

MEN: That's right, Tunnel A...

DELESSUPS: Tunnel A *is* our best alternate route, sir.

LAW: Where does it begin?

DELESSUPS: Under the pseudo-latrine in the Kommendant's office. It's a sheer drop for about 1000 yards...

LAW: Well, we can get used to that...

DELESSUPS: ...and then it gets a little nasty. But with a little luck and a full moon, I think we can make it.

LAW: Well, then, there's nothing standing in our way.

RAFFERTY: Except for the inspection, sir. We have to dispose of all the dirt before the Kommendant returns.

LAW: Dirt? What dirt?

RAFFERTY: The overflow from Tunnel Z, sir. Ten tons of red clay.

DAI: When there's red clay on the floor, you'll stay a season more...

MEN: Quiet Llewellyn...

COL. MERKIN:	Fill up the latrines with it!
RAFFERTY:	They're already filled, Colonel, sir.
COL:	Then fill up the water tower.
PROCTOR:	Filled to the brim, sir. The Kommendant's been drinking red clay for the last two weeks. He's beginning to get suspicious.
ARTUNIAN:	He's putting on weight, though. He looks good.
COL:	Well, put it in your pockets and spread it around the yard.
RAFFERTY:	If we spread it around any more, sir, we won't be able to get out of the door.
VON MIST:	Why don't we all give up?
MEN:	Nice try. Good work, Henderson.
VON MIST:	Thanks, boys.
RAFFERTY:	We can't build another pyramid. The Kommendant's taken away our chapel privileges.
MEN:	MURMUR
COL:	Wait a minute. Ashberry, weren't you a potter back in the States?
ASHBERRY:	Yes, sir, but they drafted me anyway.
COL:	How long will it take you to dispose of ten tons of red clay?
ASHBERRY:	Ready by inspection, sir.
SOUND:	KNOCKS AT DOOR
ASHBERRY:	Ready, sir.

LAW: Good show, Ashberry.

MEN: Great job...

HERBST: Achtung!...Inspection!

RAFFERTY: Hi, Kommendant. Before we begin, the men would like to present you with this case of giant souvenir ashtrays, made out of genuine red German clay.

HERBST: Well, thank you men. Ah! Memories of San Diego, 1943.

VON MIST: Two.

OSSMAN: Quiet, Henderson!

VON MIST: Thanks, boys.

HERBST: But what will I use this for?

OSSMAN: Here, have a cigar.

HERBST: Very nice. What kind is it?

OSSMAN: A Henry Clay, Kommendant.

HERBST: Oh. Well, I see you men have decorated this barracks very nicely. What is that huge red painting over there?

RAFFERTY: An original Klee, sir.

HERBST: Very good. And this life-size statue?

BERGMAN: That's our tribute to the American Fighting Man, sir — Cassius Clay.

SOUND: AUSTIN'S PIGEONS

HERBST: Oh, I didn't know you kept birds.

OSSMAN: Those are our clay pigeons.

HERBST:	All right men! Sit down!
BERGMAN:	We can't sir.
HERBST:	Why not?
BERGMAN:	The chairs haven't dried yet, sir.
HERBST:	All right! Inspection has begun. Artunian —
ARTUNIAN:	Good morning, sir.
HERBST:	Your footlocker is dusty.
ARTUNIAN:	It hasn't been glazed yet, sir.
HERBST:	Open it!
MEN:	MURMUR
ARTUNIAN:	Will somebody give me a hand? (GRUNTS)
HERBST:	What is this? A scale model of the camp?
ARTUNIAN:	No, sir. That's Clayveland, Ohio. It helps to remind me of my girl.
HERBST:	Wait a minute. What's that under your fingernails?
ARTUNIAN:	Fingers, sir.
HERBST:	Oh. Fair enough.
MEN:	MURMUR
OSSMAN:	Kommendant. Pick a number between one and ten.
HERBST:	What for?
BERGMAN:	Four it is! Bingo! You win a 118-piece unbreakable genuine clay earthenware dinner set.
SOUND:	APPLAUSE — PLATE DROPS

HERBST:	Ach du lieber. I dropped one.
OSSMAN:	Good work, Henderson.
MEN:	MUMBLE
BERGMAN:	We stand behind our guarantee. Give the Kommendant another 118-piece unbreakable genuine clay earthenware dinner set.
HERBST:	I appreciate this, boys, but what will I do with it?
LAW:	Hayakawa?
HAYA:	Hi, ya, Field Marshal.
LAW:	Give the Kommendant something to eat, lad.
HAYA:	Here is very special New Orleans Cleole tleat.
HERBST:	Yum, yum. That's very good. What is it?
HAYA:	Clay-fish.
OSSMAN:	How about some music while you eat, Kommendant?
HERBST:	You have a phonograph?
OSSMAN:	No, but we have a full-scale working clay model of our favorite singing group over in the corner.
HERBST:	Who are they?
OSSMAN:	The Nitty Gritty Dirt Band.
RECORD:	NITTY GRITTY DIRT BAND "SHIMMY LIKE MY SISTER KATE"
HERBST:	Well, everything looks pretty much in order. Beds made. Wait! What are these tablets under the bed?
RAFFERTY:	The collected works of Adam Clay-ton Powell, sir.

HERBST:	All right! Inspection's over. See you all tomorrow morning, as usual.
VON MIST:	Oh, no you won't mein Uberkommendant.
HERBST:	Henderson. What did you say?
VON MIST:	I request permission to speak to you privately, unobserved by my friends, buddies and fellow prisoners.
HERBST:	Fall in, Henderson.
VON MIST:	Eins, zwei, dreiiiiiiiiiiiiiiiiiii...!
SOUND:	FALL AND SPLASH
DELESSUPS:	So *that's* where I left tunnel E.
DAI:	When you're falling in the hole and you don't know where to go...
OSSMAN:	Quiet, Llewellyn.
HERBST:	All right now. Enough of this. What is it, Henderson?
VON MIST:	(OFF) Tonight. Midnight. Escape from Tunnel A.
HERBST:	Henderson, you ninny! You're trying to throw me off the track. Tunnel A is my latrine, and nobody uses my latrine without my permission.
LAW:	With your permission, sir...
HERBST:	You can't have it! So, there is a plot. Who's in charge here?
LAW:	Field Marshal Law here...
MARQUIS DE SADE:	According to the Geneva Convention —
RUSSIAN:	(SOVIET BABBLE)
COL. MERKIN:	Tell the little kraut I'm in charge...

HERBST: Quiet! Can't you see? Your plans will never succeed, because your leaders have feet of clay...

MEN: Good job, Ashberry... I'd like 9C... The fit's good...

HERBST: Perhaps the judicious application of some Truth Serum will get to the bottom of this. Who here is the weakest link?

LAW: Kommendant! May I remind you, according to Paragraph C, Section 14 of the Geneva Convention, no Allied prisoner of war may be willingly or unwillingly subjected to unreasonable experiment and/or torture.

MEN: APPLAUSE

LAW: Except the Armenians. Artunian! Front and center.

ARTUNIAN: Yes, sir! Ready to do or die for Fresno, sir!

HERBST: Dr. Von Filth, give him the shot.

SOUND: PETER'S PATENTED THUUUUPT

HERBST: Start counting backwards from 100.

ARTUNIAN: Derdnuh eno, enin-ytenin, thgie-ytenin, neves-ytenin, xis-ytenin, evif-ytenin...

HERBST: You are going to sleep, Artunian...your eyebrows are feeling drowsy...you are falling asleep. Now. Is there an escape plan for tonight, Artunian? I want only the Absolute Truth.

ARTUNIAN: The Absolute Truth? Form not different from emptiness, emptiness not different from form. Form is the emptiness, emptiness is the form.

HERBST: So you won't talk. All right, all camp privileges are cancelled! There will be no movies tonight!

MEN: (APPLAUSE) Good work Henderson...

HERBST:	Your escape is foiled. My latrine will be covered, even if I have to do it myself. Goodbye!
VON MIST:	Sleep tight, mein Kommendant.
OSSMAN:	Nice line, Henderson.
VON MIST:	Thanks, Von Mist.
MEN:	MUMBLE
COL. MERKIN:	All right, boys. The little kraut is onto us. It's obvious there's a stoolie here and we have only a few minutes to weed him out. Rafferty?
RAFFERTY:	Yes, sir.
COL:	Who is Lil Abner's girlfriend?
RAFFERTY:	Daisy Mae, sir.
COL:	Not you. Wilson?
PROCTOR:	Yes, sir.
COL:	Who has the power to cloud men's minds?
PROCTOR:	Oh, that's easy, sir. The Shadow.
COL:	Not you. Henderson?
VON MIST:	Ja?
COL:	Who won the World Series in 1939?
VON MIST:	Munich!
COL:	Not you. Artunian?
ARTUNIAN:	Yes, sir?
COL:	Who was the Assistant Secretary of the Interior under James K. Polk?

ARTUNIAN:	Maynard Keyes, sir?
COL:	He was the Postmaster General, you dirty rotten Nazi stoolpigeon.
MEN:	BOO HISS
ARTUNIAN:	I'm sorry, guys. I didn't know.
LAW:	Shaddup! What shall we do with him?
MEN:	(SUSTAINED MURMUR)
VON MIST:	Leave him behind.
OSSMAN:	Good thinking, Henderson.
VON MIST:	Thanks, sir.
LAW:	All right, men. Now — let's all synchronize my watch. Mickey's big hand is at one...
ARTUNIAN:	1000-1, 1000-2...
COL:	Shaddup, you yellow belly!
LAW:	Now, lads! Into the tunnel...
DAI:	(SINGING) When you're digging in the mine and we're lowered to our death...
MEN:	Let's go... Hurry up... (FADING OFF)
ARTUNIAN:	So long, guys. If any of you get to Cleveland, will you look up my girl? She's married to a real nice guy named...
MEN:	(AD LIBS IN THE TUNNEL, WHISPERS)
LAW:	Now, if Artunian's calculations were correct, we should be just below the Kommendant's office and just to the left of the movable water tower. We've got to observe strict discipline and order about this if we're going to

	get out with our lives. Ready, now. Hup, two, three, four...
PETER:	Hup two three four...
PETER AND PHIL:	Hup two three four...
DAI:	(SINGING) When you're escaping from the mines...
ALL:	(SINGING) Oh, you take the high road and I'll take the low road, and I'll be in Fresno before you...
OSSMAN:	Of the 33 men who attempted this brave escape, the records of the War Office show conclusively that all but one are now safely selling life insurance in Cleveland, Ohio.
ALL:	RIVER KWAI WHISTLE
AUSTIN:	That was THE LAST TUNNEL TO FRESNO. Our special thanks to the Walapai School of Mines and the Second World War, without which this story should never have been told. THE LAST TUNNEL TO FRESNO DOESN'T STOP HERE ANYMORE was produced in the Welsh studios of the Firesign Theatre.
DAI:	(STILL SINGING) Oh you're digging with your pick...

DAI AND RIVER KWAI SEGUE INTO OUT MUSIC CUE

TWENTY YEARS BEHIND THE WHALE

Performed live at the Magic Mushroom and broadcast on KRLA-AM on November 12, 1967. Written by the Firesign Theatre.

ORIGINAL CAST

Phil Austin as Cookie, Artunian, Chantyman, Black George

Peter Bergman as Bosun Myway, Craigcraig, O'Rian, Black Jack

David Ossman as Announcer, Startrip

Phil Proctor as Al B. Tross, Ollie, Long John, Crow's Nest, Melinda, Jolly, Pedro, Streetsinger

TWENTY YEARS BEHIND THE WHALE

RECORD: RICHARD ROGERS "SONG OF THE HIGH SEAS"

ANNOUNCER: The Firesign Theatre presents TWENTY YEARS BEHIND THE WHALE or A WINDSWEPT ROMANCE OF ADVENTURE ON THE HIGH SEAS, based on the famous adventure dramamine "Whaling" by Nat Frislin.

MUSIC UP AND UNDER

ANNOUNCER: The scene: The Shanghai Bar — a ramshackle café and house of ill-fame at the bitter end of Dock Street, Singapore — where the dregs of the sailing fraternity, men who have abandoned all hope, go for a good home-cooked meal, a pint of cheer and a friendly game of darts.

SOUND: WHISLE OF DART, THUNNNK, SCREAM

MEN: Sixteen darts in a dead man's chest — yo ho ho and a bottle of rope!

STARTRIP: Quiet down, me hearties! All right, I want all the hands of the good ship Curse of India over here in the corner.

SOUND: HANDS FALLING

STARTRIP: Belay, you jokers! Come over here and pick up your hands!

MEN:	Har har har!
AL B. TROSS:	(whistle) Polly wants a roper!
STARTRIP:	Throttle your albatross, Cookie, or I'll hang it around your neck, har har har!
AL B. TROSS:	Don't ruffle the bird! Hands off!
COOKIE:	If any of you men have a wedding you're late for, I'll tell you how I came by this bird...
AL B. TROSS:	(whistle)
STARTRIP:	You'll have plenty of time to tell your tale when you're on the High Seas tomorrow morning, har har har! All right, you men — who won the dart game?
BOSUN MYWAY:	Twas me that did it!
STARTRIP:	I suppose you think it was funny, using poor Old Blind Jim as a dart board, har har har! And tell me, Bosun Myway, how are we going to get another deckhand in time to leave on the morning flood tide when there's not a sailor of our caliber adrift between here and Singapore?
MYWAY:	This is Singapore, har har har.
STARTRIP:	Then we'll have to Shanghai somebody, har har har.
VOICE:	No, we did that last time. Let's Hong Kong somebody!
VOICE:	No, I think we should Rangoon him...
MYWAY:	This isn't the Rangoon Show! Let's send out Craigcraig.
COOKIE:	Where is that painted savage?
AL:	(whistle) Harpoon, harpoon... Pin the tall on the albatross! Braak!
STARTRIP:	Best damned harpoon in the South Seas. Is that you, Craigcraig?

CRAIG: Here I be.

COOKIE: What are you carrying, you painted savage?

CRAIG: Casket for Blind Jim.

STARTRIP: What did you carve it out of?

CRAIG: Blind Jim.

COOKIE: Clever man with a knife...

AL: (whistle) Shiver my feathers! Carve-off!

STARTRIP: Craigcraig...

CRAIG: Mmmm, Mr. Startrip.

STARTRIP: Owing to the demise of that handsome casket you're carrying, we need a new man by dawn.

CRAIG: I carve you one.

STARTRIP: There isn't enough time, har har har. You'll have to go out and find some poor, unsuspecting, wide-eyed, landlubbing dodo, har har har, with a strong back and a weak brain...

SOUND: DOOR OPENS

ARTUNIAN: Hi, guys...

STARTRIP: Too obvious.

ARTUNIAN: Well, avast and belay and button my hatches, by the cuts of your jibs I can tell you're fellow seafaring men.

BOSUN: He's pushing it.

ARTUNIAN: Well, I've got one foot in Davy Jones' locker room myself...

MEN: (mumble) Oh yeah?... He pushed it... I don't believe it.

ARTUNIAN: So why don't we sit down, do a hornpipe, and spin yarns of our cruel mistress, the Sea?

MEN: (grumble) Sure, why not? Got any yarn?

AL: Too obvious!

ARTUNIAN: Gee, it sure is colorful here. I could tell immediately that this was the sort of place where us dregs of the sailing fraternity could come for a home-cooked meal and a friendly game of darts. Say, why do they call this the Shanghai Café?

AFTER LONG PAUSE — MEN: WHAAAK!

STARTRIP: Good Job, Craigcraig. Now, lads, we've got no time to lose. By the way, what time is it?

SOUND: DING DING, DING DING, DING DING

BOSUN: Aye, Mr. Startrip — six bells. That means it's either midnight or four in the afternoon. Has anybody got a sextant?

OLLIE: Ja, ja. I got one — I'll yust take a fix on the stars...

VOICE: Drop that needle!

OLLIE: Aye, it's only my compass. Ah, let's see now — Ya! According to da position of Orion, it's gotta be May or December.

O'RIAN: Just a minute, I'll move over.

OLLIE: Step farther left, O'Rian. Yust a little more... oh oh.

O'RIAN: It's a long, long way from May to December, Ollie.

OLLIE: Hold it there, O'Rian. Let's see — en, to, tre, fire - Mr. Startrip, sir, I've got the readin', sir. Ja! It's five minutes past six bells today, sir. Ja!

STARTRIP: Then stow this healthy young volunteer, har har har,

	inside Blind Jim there and let's smuggle him on board the Curse Of India before anyone sees us, har har har. And we'll take sail... (FADING OFF)
RECORD:	RICHARD ROGERS "SONG OF THE HIGH SEAS"
SOUNDS:	CREAKS, SEA, WIND
VOICES:	Avast the foretopmast! Belay the poop deck! Shroud the mizzenmast! Joist your jib!
LONG JOHN:	Unfurl the spaniels!
SOUNDS:	BARKING
STARTRIP:	Hard to helm, steersman!
LONG JOHN:	It sure is!
STARTRIP:	Tack to starboard and luff to leeward. Course — 14 degrees left of the prow!
VOICE:	...What?
STARTRIP:	Now, pull, me hearties!
VOICE:	Where ARE your hearties, sir?
STARTRIP:	Under me laurels.
BOSUN:	Excuse me, Mr. Startrip, but the Captain wants to know if there's been any report on the sighting of Moby Budd?
STARTRIP:	I've heard nary a word of the great Paisley Beast. Not fin nor spout has broke the crest of the wave for three weeks, har har har. But I'll check with the Crow's Nest. Ahoy there!
CROW'S NEST:	Ahigh there!

STARTRIP: Give us a report!

CROW'S NEST: A report — Wow! I can see for miles and miles and miles. The wind is like 'oney 'gainst me teeth, an' the sea like a field of dancing diadems tossing me to and fro, to and fro, and when I look down — you all look like ants... I think I'm going to be sick!

STARTRIP: But what of the Great Whale?

CROW'S NEST: Yeah, what of it? (FIGHTING DOWN SICKNESS)

STARTRIP: Bosun, tell Captain Coffin, there's no word of the Whale.

BOSUN: I'll do it, but the Captain won't like it.

CROW'S NEST: I'm going to be sick! Look out below!

STARTRIP: One of you men cover the deck with newspapers.

CROW'S NEST (OFF): Get me down!

STARTRIP: Let's have an old sea shanty now, to raise our spirits!

CROW'S NEST (OFF): Help!

CHANTYMAN: (SINGS, TO "BLOW THE MAN DOWN") Blow some my way, boys, blow some my way...

O'RIAN: I didn't sign my life away on this ill-fated ship to sail the empty ocean in search of a figment of the Captain's hallabalution. I've got enough trouble following my own. Got any rope?

ANOTHER VOICE: Here.

O'RIAN: Thanks. (PUFF) Nothing like a little Manila Yella to put you straight. I can see it all — miles and miles and miles...

ANOTHER VOICE: And I can see a doomed ship with a crew of dead men and a Captain with a wooden head!

STARTRIP: Shut up, you! If the Captain ever hears you talk about his head, he'll have yours — swinging from the ardyarm — yard farm — yard bird...

CROW'S NEST: Get me down! I'm going to be sick!

STARTRIP: Put on your slickers, men, and get back to work.

CHANTYMAN: (SINGS) Give me some rope, or blow some my way...

MEN: grumble grumble

CHANTYMAN: Ollie, can I have a word with you while you're trimming the shrouds?

OLLIE: Oh, ja? Is dat what I'm doing?

CHANTYMAN: I think so. Ollie, why is it that, when the rest of the crew is so malcontent, you never complain, you're able to go about your work calmly, always with a smile in your heart? How do you do it?

OLLIE: Bah. Going to sea, lad, is like marrying to a good woman. Ja! You have to understand her cycles and her moods, as you sail the sea of life together.

CROW'S NEST: Look out! I am going to be sick!

OLLIE: Oh — let's move over here, ja. Poor fella. Now, you see yonder star? Ya, that star takes a million years to become so beautiful, and all the grumbling and impatience in the world can never hasten it one step. Ain't it beautiful?

CHANTYMAN: That's the lighthouse, Ollie.

OLLIE: Ja! Course it is. Now, look ye that star over dere is millions of years older, and there's a lesson to you, and to all of the crew. Ha ha ha! There's a time for everytin'. There's a time to sew and a time to laugh, a time to sleep and a time to know, a time to eat, a time to mutiny. Ja! Three bells in the Herring Room! I swear it's not too late.

CHANTYMAN:	I'll pass it on. Blow some my way, salties, blow some my way — (SNIFF) — three bells in the Herring Room — Blow, blow, blow some my way — (SNIFF) — Six bells in the Herring Room.
ALL:	Check!
CHANTYMAN:	Blow some my way, boyos — (SNIFF) — a quarter after herring in the check room. Blow — six mutinies after the bell in the bail room. Give me some rope or blow some my way.
MEN:	HUMMING THE SONG UNDER
ANNOUNCER:	Meanwhile, in the very same Herring Room where the mutineers are shortly to convene...
ARTUNIAN:	(MUFFLED) Oh, my head...
SOUND:	BLIND JIM CREAKS OPEN
ARTUNIAN:	...my head.
MELINDA:	Are you well, now, handsome sailor?
ARTUNIAN:	Oh, I feel like I've been blind drunk for six days.
MELINDA:	You've been inside of Blind Jim for six weeks! Let me help you out.
ARTUNIAN:	Oooooooooo!
MELINDA:	Here, smoke some herring — you'll feel better.
ARTUNIAN:	And who may you be?
MELINDA:	Oh — I'm just a simple cabin boy.
ARTUNIAN:	I should have known from your uniform — and your high heels, and your lipstick??
MELINDA:	Oh — that's to help me move more freely among the men.

ARTUNIAN: Well, you might fool me, but you can't fool me! You're not a simple cabin boy — you're a beautiful girl. And I love you!

MELINDA: Oh, I love you too, but you mustn't tell the men!

ARTUNIAN: But where am I? What happened to me?

MELINDA: You've been belaid.

ARTUNIAN: Shouldn't we tell your father?

MELINDA: Oh, no! My father's the Captain! I love him too. Many people think he's looney, but I know his mind is as solid as mahogany. As a matter of fact, it is mahogany. I love him.

ARTUNIAN: I love him too.

MELINDA: The crew calls him madman, and tyrant, and say that the decks are awash with blood. And I'll go along with that. But if you only knew my father's story. Thirteen voyages he's made in quest of the Great Paisley Whale.

ARTUNIAN: You mean Moby Budd — the fabled Hallabalution of the Seven Seas?

MELINDA: The very same. And each of those terrible voyages cost him dearly. Until last year, when he lost his head...

ARTUNIAN: Oh, that's too bad!

MELINDA: Bitten off by the great gaping jaws of that multicolored nautical terror!

ARTUNIAN: You mean — he doesn't have a head?

MELINDA: Oh, yes. Craigcraig carved him one.

ARTUNIAN: Out of what?

MELINDA: Out of his wooden leg. The one he lost the year before to Moby Budd.

ARTUNIAN: How does he walk?

MELINDA: Craigcraig carved him a new leg.

ARTUNIAN: Out of what?

MELINDA: Out of his right arm — the one he lost two years before, to that bloody Behemoth.

ARTUNIAN: Isn't it hard to steer the ship with only one arm?

MELINDA: Oh, Craigcraig carved both his arms...

ARTUNIAN: From what?

MELINDA: His abdomen.

ARTUNIAN: You mean — your father is made entirely out of wood?

MELINDA: Well, I wouldn't say that, exactly. He has a beautiful pair of ivory kneecaps Mumsey gave him for his birthday. All scrimshaw and filigree. Craigcraig carved pictures of wives waving goodbye to the fleet, and teeny weeny fishes, with teeny weeny itty bitty eyes. And the cutest little chart of the Galapagos Islands...

ARTUNIAN: The poor man. How does he stand it?

MELINDA: He lies down a lot and he sleeps like a log. Ha ha! But this year, when daddy said he was sailing off to search for Moby Budd again, I knew it was to be his fatal voyage... I pleaded with him to let me go along, so that I might curb in him his insane desire to swim alone into the mighty jaws of Moby Budd and get his body back.

ARTUNIAN: Brave boy. Er — girl. But why this confusing disguise?

MELINDA: He wouldn't let me go... He made all the silly excuses any parent would make in a similar situation — you're a girl. You're too young. You've got smallpox.

ARTUNIAN: I love you.

SOUND: DING DING DING

MEN: Here's the herring room, mumble mumble...

MELINDA: Oh. Here come the men!

ARTUNIAN: What'll we do?

MELINDA: Quick, let's hide together in Blind Jim where they're playing our song!

ARTUNIAN: Who?

MELINDA: Who else?... Country Jim and the Fish.

RECORD: COUNTRY JOE AND THE FISH "FISH CHEER"

MEN: (GRUMBLE IN) Curse of India — I feel sick — wooden headed captain.

STARTRIP: Be still, lads. Now, is everyone here? Black George? (HERE) Black Jack? (HERE) Black Comedy? (HERE) Black Top? (HERE) Black Guard? (HERE) Black Power? (HERE) Black Plague? (COUGH) What is this? A whaling ship or a pirate vessel? Well, before this voyage is over, we'll be hoisting the Jolly Roger!

JOLLY: Hey! Stop picking on me, you guys! Cut it out!

GEORGE: I'd be glad to.

STARTRIP: Leave Roger alone, Black George. We'll need every man jack we can muster.

JACK: Ah's here!

STARTRIP: Then lock the door, Black Jack, and we'll get down to business. Since the last mutiny, things have gotten worse and worse aboard the Curse of India. And we all know whose fault it is! Who has any ideas for getting rid of Captain Coffin, the old blockhead?

COOKIE:	I don't know, Mr. Startrip. Mutiny is a serious business. We could all find ourselves swinging from the arm-yard...
VOICE:	Except there ain't no rope left — we've smoked it all.
VOICE:	If he won't give us enough rope, we'll hang him!
ANOTHER VOICE:	Oh, hang it all, how are you going to hang a wooden man?
STARTRIP:	Aye, that's a good point. Who has another idea?
COOKIE:	As the oldest man aboard, and your beloved ship's cook...
MEN:	BOOOOOOOOOOOOOOOOOO
COOKIE:	Just a minute lads. I know that a diet of hardtack and lemons don't exactly fill a man's heart with song...but I am not known across the eight —
VOICE:	Seven!
COOKIE:	Seven seas as the Ancient Marinator for nothing!
VOICE:	Cookie's right, boys! He's done a good job! After all, there are only so many ways you can cook lemons. Will we ever forget his lemon meringue hardtack? It was out of sight.
ANOTHER VOICE:	Right! We threw it overboard!
VOICE:	After we ate it!
AL B. TROSS:	"I'm gonna be sick!" (whistle)
COOKIE:	Listen, lads. I've got a recipe that'll turn the trick. I'll serve him my special delicacy — steaming deep-dish termite pie!
VOICE:	Yeah, Cookie, but have you forgotten that all our deep dishes are made out of wood? The termites will be eating through the table before he can take his first bite!

STARTRIP: Craigcraig! You put him together — why can't you just take him apart?

CRAIG: Captain Coffin work of art. He promised to Lytton Center.

MEN: We want blood — he hasn't got any — we want sawdust!

SOUND: (MUFFLED SNEEZE)

STARTRIP: Was that you what sneezed, Black George?

GEORGE: It came from under my seat!

OLLIE: But men, Yeorge is sitting on Blind Yim!

STARTRIP: Shhhh! Easy, lads. Dirks ready! There's a spy in Blind Jim.

VOICES: Shh! Shh!

STARTRIP: Unbutton his coat and open him slowly!

SOUND: CREEEEEAK

VOICES: GASP

ARTUNIAN: Hi, guys!

STARTRIP: Too obvious.

ARTUNIAN: Gee, fellas, don't you remember me? You Hong Konged me in Shanghai. I mean, you Rangooned me in Hong Kong. That is — well, anyway... You probably think that the position that you see me in is somewhat compromising. But I'd like to point out that, after all, this is the Cabin Boy.

VOICE: Hi, Melindy. How's your father?

MELINDA: Pining away and making an ash out of himself, as usual. Ha ha ha!

ARTUNIAN: I couldn't help underhearing what you fellas were saying, and I'm sure you guys won't mind my speaking out, because after all — we fellow dregs of the sea must stick together like sail on a windlass. Now, as we all know, there are many traditions of the sea. One of them is to give yourself up to the Captain, body and soul, as if he were the perfect embodiment of the Supreme Being...

MELINDA: Oh, my nautical hero. That's beautiful. That's inspired!

ARTUNIAN: The other is to kill him.

MEN: Right! Yeah! Blood! Sawdust!

ARTUNIAN: But, fellow dredges, there is a third great tradition of the sea. A Captain always goes down with his ship!

VOICE: Three cheers for the Captain!

VOICE: Three cheers for the ship!

MEN: Sink, sink the ship!

STARTRIP: That's it! We'll sink the ship and the Captain will have to go down with it. Ollie, get out your auger and do a bit of work, har har har!

OLLIE: This augers not well for the Captain. You know, men — drillin' a hole in the bottom of the ship is like marrying a good woman...you have to know where to place the bit...

MEN: He's crackers...leave him alone...

BOSUN: Mr. Startrip! It's almost three and a half bells. We cross the equator at three and a half bells, and that's when the captain comes out of his cabin to stand alone on the poop deck and watch for Moby Budd.

STARTRIP: All right, everybody keep...

SOUND: DING DING DING DI

STARTRIP: That's it! We've crossed the equator. Every man jack of you get up on deck for the Captain's inspection. You too, Jack!

PEDRO: You too, man.

MEN: mumble mumble here we are get in line

STARTRIP: Captain Coffin, sir! The crew stands ready!

SOUND: SHIP'S PIPE, HICCUP, PITCHPIPE

SINGING, TO "I AM THE CAPTAIN OF THE PINAFORE"

CAPTAIN: Oh, I'm the Captain of the Curse of India —

CREW: And we all curse you too! Har har!

CAPTAIN: And be it understood, that though my head is wood, I command a worthless crew!

CREW: Har har!

RECITATIVE

CAPTAIN: Mr. Startrip! What of the Whale?

STARTRIP: We've not seen head nor tail.

CAPTAIN: Mr. Ollie! Where are the sails?

OLLIE: We smoked them!

CAPTAIN: Throw that man in chains!

AUSTIN: We smoked them too!

CAPTAIN: Chain smokers for a crew!

CREW: Har har har!

SINGING, TO "WHAT'S THE USE" (BERNSTEIN)

CAPTAIN: There's no whale,
There's no sail!
There is nothing to keep us from tempest and gale.
It's a joke
On a bloke
When your crew sends your ship up in smoke!

CREW: There's no hope
Without rope!
When you're sailing and whaling,
You've got to have rope!

RECITATIVE

CAPTAIN: But men! I have a mission! I didn't sail five thousand miles from Mystic, Connecticut, through the Panama Canal, down the Cape of Good Rope, all the way to Shanghai just to go fishing! With your permissing! Let me explain...

STREETSINGER: Und jetz, das Hans und Joni geflugen Lieder. Der Cannonen Schreibersong!

SINGING, TO "ALABAMA SONG"

CAPTAIN: Oh, show me the way to the next Paisley Whale —

CREW: Wish we were high — wish we were high!

CAPTAIN: For if I can't find the next Paisley Whale —
I tell you we must die,
I tell you we must die!

CREW: He tells us —

CAPTAIN: I tell you —

CREW: He tells us we must die! What????

CAPTAIN: Oh, Whale of the Pacific,
We're going to harpoon you!
We hate to be specific —
But that's exactly what we'll do!

LOOKOUT: Whale ho! Whale ho!

CREW: ELECTRONIC MUSIC (SOTTO VOCE)

RECITATIVE

CAPTAIN (OVER): Now that the whale has been sighted,
The crew should be rousen,
Instead of wasting your time with cheap imitations
Of Pierre Boulez and Karlheinz Stockhausen!

SOUND: PARROT WHISTLE

CAPTAIN: Now, men — into the fragile longboats! Into the fragile longboats! And though you may die, you'll never —

CREW: We'll never —

CAPTAIN: No never —

CREW: No never —

CAPTAIN: Return! Into your boats, men!

SINGING, TO "LES TRINGLES DES SISTRES TINTAIENT"

CREW: Captain tells us — get into the boat.
Captain must be making a little joke.
Captain should maybe have a little smoke!
Then he would not be such a drag!
Captain says stick it in the fish.
Captain, we do respect your wish.
Harpooning whales is not our dish!
And being drowned is not our bag!
Is not our bag! Is not our bag!

RECITATIVE

CAPTAIN: My hearty cowards! If you won't go, then I shall go alone to face the fearsome Moby Budd!

SINGING, TO "BLUE DANUBE"

CAPTAIN: That whale took my head, my leg, my arm...

MELINDA: Oh, father, don't go, you'll come to harm!

CAPTAIN: That whale took my nose, my eye, my brain!

MELINDA: Please, father, don't go — there's nought to gain!
You'll harpoon the whale —

CAPTAIN: I won't fail —

MELINDA & CAPTAIN: Or you'll/I'll die a splintery death!

SOUND: SPLASH

MELINDA: Father! Come back! (SOBS)

SINGING, TO "TOREADOR"

CREW: Old Captain Coffin's swimming toward the whale!
Will he succeed or will he fail!
Now he's swimming swiftly by its side,
And the whale doesn't see him...
Oh, yes, it sees him now!
It's turning round —
It's opening wide its — (GULP)

CREW: Hooray!

SINGING, TO "STOUTHEARTED MEN"

ALL: The Captain's been eaten,
The curse has been beaten,
The monster is swimming away!

CREW: HOORAY!
(SLOWER — WHISPERING)
But one thing's forgotten —
There's holes in the bottom —

PHIL: And soon we'll be sinking
And soon we'll be sinking
And soon we'll be sinking away!

CREW: BLUB BLUB.........

ANNOUNCER: You've just heard The Firesign Theatre's presentation of TWENTY YEARS BEHIND THE WHALE. This true story of the exploits of the Curse of India, which went down with its gallant crew off the Java Straits in 1843 —

VOICE: Two!

ANNOUNCER: Two — has yet to be told!

HUMMING SEGUE TO RECORD: BEATLES "I AM THE WALRUS"

By the Light of the Silvery
Or, The Case of the Giant Rat of Sumatra

Performed live at the Magic Mushroom and broadcast on KRLA-AM on November 19, 1967.

This radio play was later presented in a stage adaptation at the Pasadena Ice House and the Ash Grove in 1968 and at various times thereafter, including the LA Sherlockian Society. It is half the basis for the Firesign's 1973 LP "The Giant Rat of Sumatra," along with "The Fuse of Doom!"

ORIGINAL CAST

Philip Austin as Doctor Flotsom

Peter Bergman as Ottoman, Indian, Startrip, Dr. Artunian, Dr. Zygote, Sissy

David Ossman as Announcer, Raven, Masked Man, Ambassador, Alewife, Old Man, Ian, Daddy

Phil Proctor as Sureshot Homeless

BY THE LIGHT OF THE SILVERY
Or, The Case of the Giant Rat of Sumatra

RECORD: LISZT — LES PRELUDES

ANNOUNCER: The Firesign Theatre presents — The Case of the Giant Rat of Sumatra, or:

SOUND: RECORD SCRATCH-SCRATCH-SCRATCH

PHIL (SINGS): "By the Light of the Silvery..."

DOC: I remember well that foggy winter night in August 1894...

HOMELESS: 49...

VOICE: 95...

VOICE: Hike!

VOICE: Hype!

HOMELESS: Spike! Give me my shot, Doctor!

DOC: (HYPO SHOT) The great detective Sureshot Homeless was relaxing, with his feet up on the Ottoman...

OTTOMAN: Get your feet off me or I'll have the whole Turkish Army after you! Ma Shallah!

HOMELESS: Sorry, old man.

DOC: ...and contemplating the harrowing experiences he had just undergone in facing, single-handedly — with one hand only — the Giant Rat of Sumatra. The most treacherous, devastating, despicable, incongruous and intrinsically boring case we had ever undertaken. Homeless, how do you spell bummer?

HOMELESS: R.A.T. Oh, gad, Beeson, how I wish I were interrupted in the midst of these interminable memoirs by a furtive knocking on the door bringing us once again an unfathomable and unpardonably perplexing case of deception, treachery and Victorian intrigue. Then I could take another shot!

DOC: How do you spell that?

SOUND: KNOCK KNOCK

HOMELESS: Ah ha — my pleas have been answered... I deduce by that knock that on the other side of that door stands a short black man with a great beak of a nose, wearing tails and a feathered boa. Beeson, open the door and prove me correct.

SOUND: DOOR OPENS

RAVEN: Nevermore! Nevermore!

DOC: It's a raven, Homeless.

HOMELESS: Don't be fooled! It's that damned Moriarty, in one of his devilishly clever disguises. That black-hearted kangaroo will do anything for exposure.

RAVEN: Braaak!

HOMELESS: Never, Moriarity! (DOOR SLAM) Well now! I think I deserve a shot for that. (SHOT) Ow! No, Beeson, you dum-dum! Patch up my arm and get the cocaine!... Oh, I'm so terribly bored! How I long for that knock to come to deliver us...

SOUND: KNOCK KNOCK

HOMELESS: That's it, Flotsam! It's an 87-year-old man, wearing tweed underwear and calico gym socks, in possession of a rare paper — a phony medical certificate from the Walapai School of Mines.

SOUND: DOOR OPENS

DOC: Hello!

HOMELESS: Ah! It's you, Beeson! I appreciate the gesture, old man, but come in out of that mist and give me a shot.

SOUND: SHOT

HOMELESS: Ha! You missed again, you old geezer!

DOC: Ah, Homeless, things have come to a pretty pass. Back to the memoirs.

HOMELESS: Oh no — if that Giant Rat walks into my memoirs again, I'll die of boredom!

DOC: Wait a minute, Homeless! A carriage is just drawing up in front of our rooms. Two people are getting out. One is a masked lady dressed in wood, carrying a Flathead Indian with little or no regard for her personal safety. She's approaching the door...

HOMELESS: Thank goodness!

DOC: Wait! Now, they're turning round and going back to the carriage. It's pulling away. Come back, come back! We need you, whoever you are!... It's worked. They've stopped. They're getting out and walking up the steps.

HOMELESS: Yes, it's beginning! A plot at last!

SOUND: KNOCK KNOCK

HOMELESS: I deduce by that knock that just outside stands a masked lady dressed in wood, carrying a Flathead Indian with little or no regard for her own personal safety. Come in Madam! But better leave your Indian outside. I'm afraid Beeson is not entirely sympathetic with the cause of the Redman.

DOC: Let me take your mask, madam.

MAN: Thank you.

DOC: And your shoes.

MAN: Thank you.

DOC: And your dress.

MAN: Thank you.

HOMELESS: Why, without your clothes, you're naked!

MAN: Thank you.

HOMELESS: But why are you still wearing the uniform of a drum majorette in the Irish Republican Army?

MAN: I have no time to explain. I have some startling and vitally important information of a top secret nature, which I can divulge to no one. Goodbye!

HOMELESS: What?

SOUND: DOOR SLAM

DOC: Look here, Homeless — he's left his Indian.

HOMELESS: Wouldn't you?

DOC: Perhaps it's a bomb.

HOMELESS: Good thinking, Jetson. Quick, submerge him in this barrel of port. (SPLASH)

INDIAN: blub blub blub blub blub blub...

DOC: It's not a bomb.

INDIAN:	COUGH — HICCUP
HOMELESS:	Quite right! It's a drunken Redman.
INDIAN:	I'm not a Redman.
HOMELESS:	You are now — you're covered with port.
DOC:	You tawny devil.
HOMELESS:	Get his picture before he dries off, Beeson.
DOC:	Say cheese!
HOMELESS:	Get your hand away from your forehead, Indian!
INDIAN:	I was just giving you the Port Salute!
HOMELESS:	I didn't give you the Port Authority to do it.
DOC:	Look, Homeless, his disguise has washed off.
HOMELESS:	Ah ha — it's you!
INDIAN:	Yes. It's me. How did you know?
DOC:	Who's he?
HOMELESS:	It's him!
INDIAN:	How did you know?
HOMELESS:	I wrote a monograph on it once, called "It's Him".
DOC:	Where is it?
HOMELESS:	It's in the Hymn book under "Miss Elania"... Oh, give me a shot, Doctor.
SOUND:	HISS — WHISTLE & BOMB
HOMELESS:	That's not a shot, you lack-wit, that's a bomb!

DOC:	So's this script!
HOMELESS:	Quick! Submerge it in the port. (SPLASH SPLASH BLUB BLUB) Good! Now it's a port folio. Fish it out, Indian.
INDIAN:	There's a girl in here.
HOMELESS:	Of course! We have a girl in every port folio.
DOC:	What page is she on?
INDIAN:	What page are YOU on?
DOC:	Page 7.
HOMELESS:	What does it say?
DOC:	"The Giant Rat of Sumatra came at me, baring his leather fangs..."
INDIAN:	That's a Spike Milligan joke!
HOMELESS:	He's right, it's patented.
DOC:	All right, then. The Giant Rat of Sumatra came at him, baring its patented leather fangs.
INDIAN:	(DIES)
HOMELESS:	Look, Doctor. The Indian has died of boredom!
DOC:	Well, there goes another plot. "Roll out the barrel..."
VOICE:	Hard to port.
STARTRIP:	Sure is. Har har har.
SOUND:	KNOCK KNOCK
HOMELESS:	Wait! Another plot! Beeson, get the door.
DOC:	Got it!

HOMELESS:	Well, open it, you yo-yo!
DOC:	But it's ajar.
HOMELESS:	No, it's a Syrian ambassador.
DOC:	Good God! It's a Syrian ambassador in a jar!
AMBASSADOR:	Mmm mmm mmmmmmmmm!
HOMELESS:	Well, let him out, man!
SOUND:	JAR OPENING
AMBASSADOR:	Mmmmmmm — Oh, goodness gracious me! Only you could have done it, Homeless. I've been in that jam ever since Portland!
DOC:	Here, poor fellow, lie down between these two pieces of bread and we'll dry you off.
AMBASSADOR:	Ah, much better! But my throat's still sticky. Have you got anything to drink?
DOC:	Here, predictably enough — have some port.
AMBASSADOR:	Mmmmm, that's good! What is it?
HOMELESS:	Indian port.
AMBASSADOR:	Indian port?
HOMELESS:	Yes, it's been cured in Indians.
AMBASSADOR:	Any port in a jam.
INDIAN:	Page 9!
HOMELESS:	Ah, we've made it! Now, Mr. Ambassador, what's this you said about someone stealing the moon?
AMBASSADOR:	But I haven't said that yet.

HOMELESS:	Well, say it.
AMBASSADOR:	Gentlemen: "Someone has stolen the moon."
DOC:	What did you say?
AMBASSADOR:	You may scoff...
DOC:	Thank you.
ALL:	COUGH
AMBASSADOR:	...but three years ago, the Assyrian government — or a Syrian government — was given 8 billion dollars by the United States to burn wheat and flood Damascus, thereby creating the largest international sponge ranch west of Beirut. With the remaining 8 billion, we decided to enter the space race. We gathered together the finest scientist in the country and, through a German interpreter, ascertained how to build a mighty rocket. Our first shot landed successfully on London. After paying off the insurance, we had just enough money left to send our scientist to the moon. But then, a strange thing happened... We missed!
HOMELESS:	There's nothing strange about that.
AMBASSADOR:	We didn't think so either. We've missed before and we'll miss again. Then we discovered that we hadn't missed the moon. The moon had missed us.
DOC:	That's absurd!
HOMELESS:	No, it's insane!
VOICE:	No, it's a super-plot!
DOC:	It'll look great in your memoirs, Homeless.
HOMELESS:	Get on with it, Ambassador.
AMBASSADOR:	The last message we received from our scientist was

that the moon was definitely not there! Mr. Homeless, will you take the case?

HOMELESS: What a challenge! Of course I'll take the case...

AMBASSADOR: All right then! Here it is...

HOMELESS: Why this is a case of smallpox! Couldn't you get anything bigger?

AMBASSADOR: I'm sorry. That's all they had.

HOMELESS: Well, it'll be fine for a pox lunch. Put it in the freezer next to the mumps. Doctor, we're off!

VOICE: You sure are.

TRANSITION: MUMBLE MUMBLE

DR. ARTUNIAN: Gentlemen, gentlemen! The 23rd Annual Emergency Meeting of the Royal Armenian Academy of Arts and Sciences will please come to order! Mr. Homeless, I believe you have a report.

DOC: BANG!

ARTUNIAN: Stop that, Doctor!

HOMELESS: Thank you. Hold him down. Gentlemen: The moon has disappeared!

VOICE: Rubbish!

VOICE: Nonsense!

VOICE: Dogmatic twaddle!

HOMELESS: No! True! Dr. Alewife, as Ringbearer of the Royal Lithuanian Yacht Club at Stanes-On-Seat, have you noticed any significant change in the tide table?

ALEWIFE: Yes, it's disappeared.

VOICES: MUMBLES

ALEWIFE: No, sorry — I was sitting on it. But we have noticed that the tides are running a bit high for this time of year. Switzerland, for instance, is now an island... (MURMUR) ...the salmon are spawning in the main streets of Omaha... (MURMUR) ...and we've opened up a new branch office in Atlantis. (MURMUR OF APPROVAL) Other than that, nothing of significance.

VOICES: Balderdash... Nonsense...

VOICE: I'm sure that can all be explained scientifically!

VOICES: Marsh gas... Fraud... It'll never get off the ground...

VOICES: Painless surgery, ha! Talking over wire, humbug!

HOMELESS: Dr. Zygote of the Royal Balinese Gynecological Society and Marching Band, have you any information pertaining to the subject at hand?

ZYGOTE: Odd you should mention it.

HOMELESS: Odd you should say so.

ZYGOTE: As you all know, the moon governs the monthly cycle of egg production in the female. I have a working model over here...

VOICE: Watta tomato!

ZYGOTE: No, sir! It's an egg!

VOICE: And you're an egg man!

DR. ZYGOTE: And you, sir, are a walrus! Googoo catchoo!

VOICE: Gezundheit!

ZYGOTE: Dankeshoen. Now, if it were true that the moon had disappeared, there would naturally be a significant decrease in the birthrate of bunny rabbits. But I am not the man to give you the last word on bunny rabbits, and I wouldn't if I could.

VOICE: Can you?

ZYGOTE: No. So, I must turn to my distinguished colleague, who, as the Director of the Royal Australian Geophysical Bunny Rabbit Count, is not only the world's only validated expert on bunny rabbits, but is himself a bunny rabbit. Let's get the cute little fellow up here. Gentlemen — Professor Marsh Hare!

SOUND: APPLAUSE — COUGHS

ZYGOTE: Professor Hare? Oh, Hare, are you here? Where's Hare?

VOICE: Hare? Hare? No, not here.

VOICE: (SINGING, TO "OVER THERE") Where is Hare? Where is Hare?

ALL: (SING) "And we won't come back 'til we've found Professor Hare." Hey!

ZYGOTE: He's not here!

ALEWIFE: Gentlemen! Professor Hare's disappearance can only mean one thing — the moon *is* gone! There's nothing more I can say. I will now turn over the podium.

SOUND: CRASH

DOC: He's turned over the podium!

HOMELESS: Dr. Beeson, we have no time to lose! Get that podium off your stomach and let's be off!

DOC: Homeless, this case presents the greatest challenge of your career. What's your next step to be?

HOMELESS: A fox trot.

DOC: May I have this dance?

VOICES: WHISTLE "BLUE DANUBE"

HOMELESS: Charmed! One — 2 3 4 — I want you to — 3 4 — go out and find out everything you can about the moon — 2 3 4...

DOC: But, Homeless! The moon has disappeared!

HOMELESS: Then try the British Museum. 3 4 5 — Beeson, you mad dog, you're doing the Continental!

DOC: But what are you doing?

HOMELESS: Let that be my little secret. We'll meet at midnight tonight, on the heath where the moon was last seen. Do you understand?

DOC: No.

HOMELESS: Good! Adieu.

VOICE: Gesundheit!

DOC: Good night! Parting, I might add, is such sweet sorrow, that I shall say good-night till it be morrow. By yonder blessed moon I vow...

HOMELESS: O, swear not by the moon, the inconstant moon, that monthly changes in her circled orb...

DOC: What shall I swear by... ?

RECORD: BEATLES "MISTER MOONLIGHT"

SOUND: WIND

DOC: It's well past midnight, and damned cold on this blasted heath. Where is Homeless?

SOUND: DOG HOWLING

DOC: Oh, that horrid hound of the Bakersfield, it sends chills down me throat!

OLD MAN:	Excuse me, sir.
DOC:	What? What's that? You gave me a fright!
OLD MAN:	Here, take two, they're very small.
DOC:	Thank you.
OLD MAN:	I'm naught but an old, blind, crippled shepherd, and I've lost my way. I was wondering if you might have found it?
DOC:	No, I haven't, but here's your fright back. BOO!
OLD MAN:	Boo? I never touch the stuff. It makes you blind, you know. Could you tell me the way to the city of London?
DOC:	Aha! Homeless, you wily devil. Thank goodness you're here!
OLD MAN:	I am?
DOC:	I'd know that withered limb and glass eye anywhere, Homeless. And you used that crutch in "The Case of the Rubber Crutch". It was very funny.
OLD MAN:	What — What? Sir, where's London, sir?
DOC:	Come now, Homeless. Give me that silly white beard, and that withered limb, and that blank stare... (SCUFFLE)
OLD MAN:	Look out! You're pushing me near the heath cliff!
DOC:	My name isn't Cliff! Sit ye down, Father Homeless!
OLD MAN:	My name isn't Homeleeeeeeess...! (FALLS OFF CLIFF)
DOC:	Poor old devil. Oh, well, at least I have his beard to keep me nose warm.
SOUND:	ROCK — WHOOSH — SLAM

DOC: Ow! Who threw that rock? Why, there's a note attached! A five-pound note! I can buy a bigger rock, and get a trade-in on this one...

HOMELESS (OFF): Put me down, Doctor!

DOC: Is that you, Homeless? Where are you?

HOMELESS (OFF): I am the rock.

DOC: Sure — and I am an island.

HOMELESS (OFF): Let me show you, Batson. I'll just rip off this disguise... (ON-MIKE) Ha!

DOC: Damned clever, Homeless! I didn't recognize you.

HOMELESS: No, you took me for granite! Now, Beeson, what did you find out at the British Museum?

DOC: My library card has expired. What about you, Homeless?

HOMELESS: Beeson, this spot is exactly where the moon was last seen. Look what you're standing on.

DOC: My feet.

HOMELESS: No, you're standing on my feet! Get off! Can't you see those two parallel tracks?

DOC: (TSK) Homeless, you should be ashamed of yourself.

HOMELESS: No! Not my arm! On the ground!

DOC: Oh, yes. What do you make of them?

HOMELESS: Evolutionary, my dear Beeson. They were produced by the parallel wheels of a circa-1890 Sicilian dog-cart, with brass trimmings and faded roses painted on the sides, loaded to the brim with hero sandwiches and pretzels.

DOC:	Amazing, Homeless! You can tell all that from these tracks alone?
HOMELESS:	Don't be silly! I was caught in its wheel when I was disguised as a rock. The cart is parked over there.
DOG:	HOWLS
DOC:	Good! I was getting hungry anyway. Here, Homeless, have a sandwich.
DOG:	HOWLS
HOMELESS:	Thank you. Pay that Italian dog. And don't throw away the paper that sandwich was wrapped in. It might be a clue. Aha! Just as I suspected — it's a page from the Personals section of Mechanics Illustrated! Read this.
DOC:	"Handy AC-DC fix-it man desires electrical and emotional outlets. No cranks or phonies. Send schematic drawing..."
HOMELESS:	No! Let me read it. Yes, here it is. "For sale: Slightly damaged Russian, American and Syrian lunar probes. Many valuable parts, including feet, mirrors, sensors and solar batteries. Original cost in the millions, yours for a farthing."
DOC:	Why, Homeless — what can this mean?
HOMELESS:	Beeson, the person who wrote this ad has the moon.
DOC:	Fantastic! But how shall we ever find him? I know, I know. You'll probably track him down by such inscrutable clues as the typeface the ad is set in.
HOMELESS:	Yes, it's Art Nouveau Bodoni, only available in Northern Scotland. Look at this watermark.
DOC:	Why, it's still wet!
HOMELESS:	Exactly! Glasgow! By the total absence of any linen

fibers in the paper, it's obviously from the Mumsworth District.

DOC: Amazing!

HOMELESS: And look at the peculiar irregularities in the spacing of these letters. Quite obviously, the typesetter's table was tilted!

DOC: Sunny Goodge Street!

HOMELESS: Exactly! And due to the misspelling of the word "walrus", the man who wrote this probably lives in the third house from the bottom of the hill.

DOC: Unbelievable! And his name, Homeless?

HOMELESS: Alimentary, Batson! George Maughmsey.

DOC: Homeless, you're incredible! How do you do it? How could you possibly deduce that?

HOMELESS: Nothing to it. It's here in black and white at the bottom of the ad — "George Maughmsey, 3 Sunny Goodge Street, Mumsworth, Glasgow, Northern Scotland." Eureka! Page 21! Now into the dog cart and let's be off! We haven't got a page to lose! On you huskies, avant!...

SOUND: DOGS HOWLING

MUSIC: DONNA DIANA OVERTURE

SOUND: DOGS PANTING

HOMELESS: Down, you Italian curs! Basta, basta!

DOC: This must be the place, Homeless. See that sign? "Maughmsey's Ye Olde Exotique Curio and P.J. Probe Shoppe."

HOMELESS: That's "Lunar Probe Shoppe", you foole! Let's get out of that, and go in.

SOUND:	TINKLING BELL — DOOR OPENS
IAN:	Good evening, gentlemen. Might I interest you in a genuine Abyssinian curd bowl?
DOC:	Why it's beautiful! Could you gift wrap it?
IAN:	No, I'm sorry — we're out of rabbits just now.
HOMELESS:	What did you say?
IAN:	I won't repeat it. How do you like this genuine 1884 fancy East Indian curry? Lord Kitchener brought it up continually during his last campaign...
HOMELESS:	No. Actually, I am in the market for a lunar probe.
IAN:	Ah. One moment, sir... Sissy?
SISSY:	What is it, Ian?
IAN:	It's the fuzz. They're on to Daddy!
SISSY:	Ooooooo! I knew this would happen. Well, gentlemen, you might as well know it all. Come back here in the storage room and we'll talk it over. Watch your head, sir!
HOMELESS:	Why, I don't know what you're talking about, young lady. I haven't had a shot for hours.
DOC::	What a lot of hardware! What's that?
SISSY:	That's the Lunik 4.
HOMELESS:	And what's that?
IAN:	The Assyria 2.
DOC:	Look out, Homeless!
SOUND:	DDDRRRRRRRRRRR
HOMELESS:	I say! What was that?

SISSY: The Surveyor 15... It just took 8000 photographs of your left foot! You'll have the prints in half an hour.

DOC: Actually, little lady, we're more interested in your *father's* prints. Aha!

HOMELESS: Oho!

IAN:: Oh-oh!

SISSY: OOOoooooooo! (BURSTS INTO TEARS)

DOC: We didn't mean to make you cry, but we have every reason to believe that your father has copped the moon!

SISSY: Ian, they know!

IAN: Quiet, Sissy! Pull yourself together!

SISSY: Hunnnnh!

IAN: That's much better. You were spreading out all over the room. Most distasteful!

SISSY: Ian, we'll have to tell them.

IAN: Don't say a word until you speak to your lawyer!

SISSY: But, you're my lawyer.

IAN: Then let me give you a piece of advice.

SISSY: Thank you. Would either of you gentlemen like one?

DOC: No, thank you. I've just had a bit of a fright.

HOMELESS: Put mine in a doggy bag for later. Now let's get back to business. Where were we?

SISSY: Page 24. On which I say — ahem — "It all began about three years ago, when Daddy, who fancies himself — when there's no one around — something of an astronomer, turned his teleidoscope on the moon.

And then, for some strange reason, he became obsessed with that pale mistress of the sky. He began stealing it in a small way — once a month. Oddly no one seemed to notice. Then he became bolder and bolder..."

HOMELESS: Yes, I remember meeting him when I was a rock.

IAN: He kept it then for longer and longer periods of time. We never knew what he did with it. I warned him that people would begin to notice, but he took no heed.

SISSY: He hadn't taken any since Mother got him off the stuff.

HOMELESS: That reminds me, Beeson. It is time for my shot!

SOUND: BANG

HOMELESS: Aha! You blind fool, you've missed again!

SISSY: Yes, and just look at the hole you've made in the back wall of the shop!

DADDY: rrrrrmmmmmrrrrr

DOC: What was that?

HOMELESS: Come, Doctor, and look through this hole. What do you see?

DOC: A large, white pitted object!

SISSY: Oh, Ian! He's discovered the large, white pitted object in our back yard. Daddy will be furious!

HOMELESS: Come, Beeson. Let's get to the bottom of this.

SOUND: DOOR

DOC: Homeless, do you realize that that large, white pitted object is?

HOMELESS: Yes, Beeson. It's incredible! Do you realize that over half a million babies were born today, all over the world, with their sun in Aquarius and their Moon in Glasgow?

DADDY: Here you! Keep your filthy hands off me moon! You'll smudge it!

SISSY: Daddy!

HOMELESS: Just a second, old man. What do you mean, your moon? The moon belongs to everyone.

ALL (SINGING): "And the best things in life are free..."

DADDY: So you sing. But what do they do? Do they look at it? Do they make love under it? Do they write songs about it? No! They hurl dirty great machines at it — that come down in a whoosh of flame, scorching its tender skin, wounding it, and wreaking havoc in the Sea of Tranquility! Then they scrape away at it, and make it bleed, and then take pictures of the carnage they have done! Well, that's all in the past now, because I'm taking good care of it, me!

HOMELESS: Sir, in the name of the Queen, I must ask you to return the moon to its rightful place in the heavens.

DADDY: Did you say — the Queen?

HOMELESS: Did I say what?

DADDY: The Queen.

HOMELESS: Yes, I did. You just said it too.

DADDY: What?

HOMELESS: The Queen.

DADDY: Oh. In that case, as a gentleman, I can only comply. However, there is one condition.

HOMELESS: What is that, old man?

DADDY:	That I be allowed to go back with it to protect it from the madness of this world.
SISSY:	But, Daddy, how will you live?
DADDY:	Unpretentiously. Goodbye, children!
SISSY & IAN:	Goodbye, Daddy.
DOC:	Well, Homeless, another case has been solved by your brilliant... Homeless? Homeless?
HOMELESS:	(OFF) I'm off with the moon, Doctor!
DOC:	But — but why?
HOMELESS:	(OFF) Because I'm going to solve the greatest case of my career — the Mystery of the Universe! (SINGS) "Ah, sweet mystery of life, at last I've found thee..." (AD LIB UNDER, INCREASINGLY UNINTELLIGIBLE)
DOC:	And so, Homeless had solved the Mystery of the Missing Moon, only to embark on an even greater quest. I did not know if I would ever see my friend again — and I didn't much care, because I still had, as a memory, eight thousand 8-by-10 glossies of his left foot. So, I returned to Bakersfield Street to finish off the rest of my days, bored to tears with cleaning up after the Giant Rat of Sumatra — which occasionally reminded me very little of the time when, on the third of June, another sleepy, dusty Delta day, I was out chopping cotton and Homeless was bailing hay...
RECORD:	DOORS "ALABAMA SONG"
ANNOUNCER:	The Firesign Theatre has just presented BY THE LIGHT OF THE SILVERY. Any similarity to persons or planets living or dead is a stroke of purely accidental genius. Ah! Here we are, bottom of page 27. Good night, folks!

THE SWORD AND THE STONED

Performed live at the Magic Mushroom and broadcast on KRLA-AM on December 3, 1967.

This piece was adapted for the stage and presented at the Ice House and the Ash Grove and at the May 1968 Renaissance Pleasure Faire.

ORIGINAL CAST

Phil Austin as Sir Lee, Sir Raglio, King Arthur, Innkeeper

Peter Bergman as Sir Vile, Sir Cuitous, Sir Mount, Brother Burana, Sir Rendipity

David Ossman as Announcer, Sir Perfluous, Sir Realist, Sir Tain, Merlin, Sir Mount, Shepherd

Phil Proctor as Festoon, Sir Valence, Brother Rat, Sir Prize, Sir Plus

THE SWORD AND THE STONED

THE KNIGHTS: (SINGING) Hey, nonny, nonny, nonny... (CONTINUES UNDER)

ANNOUNCER: Ladies and gentlemen, The Firesign Theatre presents THE SWORD AND THE STONÉD — a Romantic Legend of Olden Tymes.

THE KNIGHTS: (SINGING) Nonny, nonny, nonny, no! Hey!

FESTOON PLUCKS HIS LUTE AND SINGS

FESTOON: In days of old, when lead was gold,
In the reign of Arthur our King,
The Round Table Knights were gathering mold,
But the times they are a changing!

THE KNIGHTS: Aaah! Sing us something bawdy! Something dirty! Something with a little pie in it! Do it properly!

FESTOON: My mistress' eyes are like the sun,
Her boots of Spanish leather,
I put my finger on her lump
With a hey nonny... (AD LIB)

SIR PERFLUOUS: Ah! The minstrel wanes his singing song too weakly, methinks. Forthwith, I would propose to stuff his nose with snuff enough, and divers joints of righteous stuff. And thus, in sooth, pursue the course of Holy...

SIR VILE: Give the Fool a joint of henbane!

FESTOON: I saw a crystal ship on a mountain eight

Miles high and with a little help from
My friends I crossed the Strawberry Fields
And Elaine in the Lake with diamonds!

SIR PERFLUOUS: Ah! Methinks the minstrel sings with tongue of gold, and in his honeyed words doth cast a spell...

SIR LEE: Yeah! Rip out his tongue!

SIR VILE: Hooray for the minstrel! Kill him!

SIR VALENCE: Knights! Knights! Better we should come to order than to blows!

SIR CUITOUS: Blow some my way!

SIR VALENCE: Gentle sire! Good knights!

SIR REALIST: Good night, Sir Valence.

SIR VALENCE: Come back to the Round Table, Sir Realist! Noble Lords — since last we met, a score of moons have waned and set...

SIR LEE: Aye! Since last the moon hath waned, we have not scored!

SIR VILE: Let's go on a quest for henbane!

SIR VALENCE: Not now! For we have gathered here in Court to give King Arthur good report of all the deeds of valor we have done since last we met.

SIR TAIN: You bet!

SIR VALENCE: And so forthwith, let's go in order round the Table Round.

THE KNIGHTS: (SINGING) Here we go round the Table Round,
The Table Round, the Table Round,
Here we go round the Table Round,
So Middle in the Ages...

SIR VALENCE: Sir Vile! Thou's first thy deeds shall give of good account, thereof. Er...first, that which account that thou of...indeed, for us... What's happening?

SIR VILE: I just returned from quest in Westmoreland, a horrid place where killing time and dragons is the fashion. And may I to your anxious ears report that upon the bloodied field of valor, by veritable count, a full fourteen great behemoths were laid full low! My own losses were light...

SIR RAGLIO: Sir Light is dead?

SIR VILE: And of that count mine own hand did slew not two but three great hornéd Gregorian beasts...

SIR TAIN: Papal bull!

SIR VILE: Are you accusing me of playing beast bull, Sir Tain?

SIR TAIN: I myself did hear the frightful howling of the deaded beasts as they did hang upon your lance, Sir Vile. Dragons, indeed! A hideous sound to hear whilst you were slewing — the poor beasts mooing! Let's hear some booing!

THE KNIGHTS: Boo! I'm out of boo!

SIR VALENCE: I pray you be still! Good knights!

THE KNIGHTS: (SINGING) Good knights, Elaine, Good knights, Elaine,
I'll see you in my lake...

SIR VALENCE: And now, young Sir Raglio! Recount to us your maiden voyage of valor.

SIR RAGLIO: Well, I tried again, guys. I put another year into it. I think she noticed me this time, 'cause I got real close to the tower — which, by the way, is a really remarkable piece of architecture. The Magician who keeps her enthralled has really good taste!

SIR VALENCE: Did you rescue her?

SIR RAGLIO: No, but I did talk to her father, and I think he's beginning to see things my way — that I can basically offer her more than being condemned to sit in a tower for a thousand years, wrapped in thorns, up to her neck in boiling oil, surrounded by a horde of imaginary trolls and gibbering dwarfs. I got a lock of her hair, though...

THE KNIGHTS: Big deal! Hair freak!

SIR VALENCE: Well spaked, Sir Raglio! Now speak, Sir Mount. Who have you met upon the Field of Honor this twelvemonth past?

SIR MOUNT: I have met in dubious battle and bested the Black Knight!

THE KNIGHTS: Bravo! Hear hear! Where where?

SIR MOUNT: And the Brown Knight, and the Electric Blue Knight, and Shirley Knight and Twelfth Knight and Opening Knight! And I have the good reviews to prove it, too!

SIR PLUS: You jest!

SIR MOUNT: No, I joust!

SIR LEE: You're juiced!

SIR MOUNT: Only on my mother's side!

SIR VALENCE: Silence, knights!

THE KNIGHTS: (SINGING) Silence knights. Holy knights...

SIR VILE: That was the 7:00 o'clock News...

SIR VALENCE: Enough! Beshrew yourselves. Here cometh the King, with his sorcerer Merlin close on his behind.

SOUND OF TRUMPET CALLS

KING ARTHUR: Good morning, my noble knights!

THE KNIGHTS: Good morning to you! Good morning to you!
We're all in our placings
With bright, shiny facings,
Good morning King Arthur, good morning to you!

ARTHUR: Your raucous behavior hath stained the scutcheon of my bounteous hospitality. Get ye gone! Beshrew!

THE KNIGHTS: What? We are gone. I left my shrew outside.

ARTHUR: Out, out! Damned knights...

THE KNIGHTS FADE OFF, LEAVING ARTHUR AND MERLIN ALONE

ARTHUR: Oh, Merlin! Heavy times have fallen on the court.

MERLIN: Aye, the times are heavy, sire.

ARTHUR: Heavy lie the times.

MERLIN: Upon the court.

ARTHUR: Yea! Heavy!

MERLIN: Tis heavy, sire.

ARTHUR: Tis! Tis...heavy...

FESTOON ENTERS, TWANGING HIS PERFIDIOUS LUTE

ARTHUR: Ah, Festoon, my wise fool. Come hither. Sit upon my feet and stroke your limpid lute, til joyous sounds do flood mine ear and assuage my sinking spirits.

FESTOON: What?

ARTHUR: Sing something funny, lad!

FESTOON: (SINGING) Lie heavy, lie heavy!
Upon the court,

And the times, festering times
They are a heavy...

ARTHUR: Ha, ha! Thank you, good fool! Your obscure wit oft doth mask the fettered truth.

FESTOON: The truth tis true, doth lie in lies.

ARTHUR: Ha, ha! But, boy — does not the truth take troth when married to her lying lies?

FESTOON: Aye, merry, sire. And merry times do oftimes lie between the truth, and truth itself belies, between the courtiers and their Queen!

ARTHUR: Queen, sayest thou, fool?

FESTOON: What Queen?

ARTHUR: What, fool?

MERLIN: What are you talking about, you ninnies?

FESTOON: Why, Merlin, aged sooth, in truth, forsooth — the lie that lies between the truth — it lies between a lying lady's lying thighs!

MERLIN: Oh, shut up, you odorous twit!

ARTHUR: Festoon, your serious wit doth now obscure the dreadful business of our court. Two words, dear fool, and then anon — get out! Begone!

FESTOON: Aye, sire. Let be gones be be gones.

MERLIN: Off with you, boy!

FESTOON: (SINGING) I'm off, you mean old wizard,
You rotten old wizard, you fraud...

MERLIN: I'm glad he's gone. He smells.

ARTHUR: So doth the court, entire of itself. It reeks of dalliance, cowardice, braggadocio, and...

MERLIN: Henbane, sire.

ARTHUR: Ever since Sir Beau Croatian, the Syrian Ambassador, did visit on our once sober shores this wicked weed, my knights have paisleyed up their armor and taken to the wearing of the Venerable Bead. Troubled lies the head that's wreathed in smoke and not in gold. Oh, Merlin, how can we ventilate with winds of change this sorry state?

MERLIN: A test.

ARTHUR: You jest.

MERLIN: Tis best!

ARTHUR: I'll send them out to face the fearful Turk!

MERLIN: They'd lose!

ARTHUR: I should have guessed. Then what do you suggest?

MERLIN: A quest.

ARTHUR: A quest? A quest? That's blessed!

MERLIN: A quest that's blessed at your behest!

ARTHUR: I know not what to do, I must confess.

MERLIN: Oh, what a mess! No! Arthur, leave off rhyming. It's bad for your soul and worse for your timing. I think I may have the answer, sire. Send off your fallen knights to search for that most wondrous and invisible of relics — the Holy Goose!

ARTHUR: The Holy Goose! Tis done! They'll leave at dawn. Let's to the Monks and have their orders drawn.

SOUND: LOUD KNOCKING

ARTHUR: (MUFFLED, OFF) Hola! Brother Rat! Are you within?

BROTHER RAT: Knock, knock! Let sleeping Monks lie, can't you? Knock, knock, knock! Is that you, Luther? You trouble-maker! Nailing up my oak door with those illegible theses of yours? They're not even illuminated! Do you know what you're doing, Luther? Laying the foundation for 500 years of bloody civil war, the Protestant Ethic, the Counter Reformation, Torquemada, the Industrial Revolution, and Paul Tillich? You're setting brother against brother, seminary against seminary, fund drive against fund drive, all because of Simony??? And the selling of Indulgences???

ARTHUR: (MUFFLED, OFF) It's the King!

BROTHER RAT: Martin Luther King! That's even worse, wait and see!

MERLIN: No! It's King Arthur!

BROTHER RAT: Oh! The King! Why didn't you say so? Let the door be opened! Sing, boys, sing!

THE MONKS: (PLAINCHANT) E pluribus unim... In vino veritas... Galia in tres partes divisa est... In hoc Signor Wences...

ARTHUR: Brother Rat! I have a holy order for your Holy Order to illuminate.

BROTHER RAT: Oh, goody, good, good! Let me get you my Illuminati, Brother Carmen Burana. Burana!

BROTHER BURANA: (OFF) I'm in the ergot cellar, scraping mold, Brother Rat!

BROTHER RAT: Come on up! We've got a manuscript for you to illuminate!

BROTHER BURANA: (ENTERING) Oh, goody, good, good! Hello, King! Pardon my appearance, sire, but I've been bottling belladonna. This manuscript of yours, how does it start?

ARTHUR: In the name of the King...

BROTHER BURANA: Oh! That starts with an "I" — you can't do anything with an "I" — oh, you can wrap a couple of snakes around it, but... Listen! Can't you arrange for a "W"? Like "We the people"? I've had this "W" on my mind for a long time, now. Imagine this: The zodiac, the changes of the seasons, all happening over this beautiful countryside, with a farmhouse and stubbles of corn and little tiny deer and tiny sheep with teeny weeny eyes and falcons flying and a lot of people on a pilgrimage going from left to right and a Wife in a Bath, surrounded by a map of the Terra Incognita! No perspective and plenty of factory extras! How does it sound?

ARTHUR: Fine, but I have to have it...

BROTHER BURANA: And behind the "W" in reverse is the Chinese reflection of the entire event, plus a history of the Great Plague in all its beauty, and a Child's Garden of Alchemy...

ARTHUR: Fine! But I need it tomorrow morning!

BROTHER RAT: Well, a job of this magnitude might take us 40 score years, your sinus — but with the effort of 50 score monks, a gallon of albumen, a hogshead of clean henbane, and the Help of God, I think we can score it. Amen!

ARTHUR: Done! Come, Merlin, let's go ask the Watchmen what of the knights...

THE KNIGHTS FADE ON SCENE, BABBLING

ARTHUR: My noble knights! You are gathered here by the grace of God, so that I may charge you with a quest of great and holy purpose.

THE KNIGHTS: Sounds like work... What a drag... Back to the locksmith... I've got to polish my armor...

ARTHUR: Sir Prize! Thou shalt read the Proclamation. Here.

SIR PRIZE:	W...www...ww...Wow! Look at this little teeny sheep with the little teeny eyes, and this little family dog down here...
SIR VILE:	Hey, we could make a poster out of that for our next w ball!
ARTHUR:	Enough!
MERLIN:	I'll read it! W...hen in the course of knightly events, it behooves the Royal We to rid the kingdom of you bums. Therefore, you are sent forth upon a Holy Mission as far south as possible, over impassible mountains, impenetrable forests and implacable deserts, on an impossible Quest — in search of the Holy Goofe. Oh! Holy Goose. This is nicely lettered, Arthur.
ARTHUR:	Any quest-ions?
SIR LEE:	I'm getting out of here, me!
SIR PLUS:	I've got to go to the knight school!
SIR MOUNT:	I don't fealty too good!
ARTHUR:	You fealty traitor!
SIR CUITOUS:	Grail, sí, Goose, no!
THE KNIGHTS:	Hell no, we won't go!
ARTHUR:	And what of you three there? And the Fool?
THE FOUR:	Mmmmmmmmmmmmm...
MERLIN:	It seems that wily Sir Cumference has gagged and chained them to the table! I smell foul play. And the Fool besides!
ARTHUR:	They're hired! Those three shall go on a questing! I hereby commission you — Sir Raglio, Sir Perfluous and Sir Vile — Knights of the Holy Goofe...

MERLIN: Goose, Arthur.

ARTHUR: Ah! Goose! When are these monks going to learn to fpell?

MERLIN: Send the Fool along. The dog!

ARTHUR: I wouldn't send that dog out with knights like this!

MERLIN: Then knight him!

SIR RENDIPITY: No! Dog the others!

KING ARTHUR: Quiet, Sir Rendipity! Fool! You a knight shall be. Get me my sword... That's my sward... With wit and song and divers tongues, you've cheered my soul in days both dim and bright. For Hardy Service, be so named, and wreath thy brows with laurel bows! Arise, Sir Laureled Hardys, Knight! Now, get lost!

THE KNIGHTS: So long, suckers! Hey, Sir Vile! I'll tell your wife — just leave me the key! Yeah, leave me half a key!

ARTHUR: And as for the rest of you — false knights! You'll go a searching for the Cold Turkey on the Guernsey Isles! Now, get thee gone, whilst I listen to my favorite band of minstrels — the Jim Questing Goofe Band!

RECORD: JIM KWESKIN AND THE JUG BAND "SOMEBODY STOLE MY GAL"

SOUND — HORSES, CONTINUING UNDER

NARRATOR: And so, that very night, our four questors broke their first ground in search of the Holy Goose... There was Sir Raglio in armor shining like the moon...

SIR RAGLIO: Hey guys — boy, isn't this fun, the four of us being out here together, a feeling of camaraderie riding along in the moonlight?... Hey, guys?... Fellahs? Where are you?... Guys?

NARRATOR: Sir Perfluous, writing his memoirs...

SIR PERFLUOUS:	"When first I read it out upon the amber leaves of grain"... No, no... "And miles to go before I sleep"... No... "It's a long way to Northumberland"... No...
NARRATOR:	And fierce Sir Vile, bearing his lance, jogged grimly on behind his shield of steel.
SIR VILE:	Look what a fine figure is my noble steed galloping so solitary in yonder moonlight...hey wait a minute...I must have fallen off. Horsie! Horsie!
NARRATOR:	And of course, Sir Fool.
FESTOON:	We four knights in armor bright Move swiftly towards our fate No wizard's wand or army's might Can stay us from the land of — nonny nonny nonny — Does anybody know what rhymes with "lost"?
SIR PERFLUOUS:	I have here an Ancient Map, much used by travelers of yore. Twas give me by bold Sir Vey, before we left our shore.
SIR RAGLIO:	Oh, neato! Is it a good map?
SIR PERFLUOUS:	Yea, verily. It doth represent each and every road, way, path, fen, bog, hill, hummock, city, stableyard and marsh within its compass. It is indeed a goodly map — of French Somaliland.
SIR VILE:	Oh! Vey's map! It will not help us here, south of North Umberland.
FESTOON:	North of South Umberland.
SIR VILE:	As the case may be.
SIR RAGLIO:	Look! Up ahead! An Inn! Do you think they'll let us in?
SIR VILE:	Of course. We're in with the Inn crowd. What ho! Innkeeper!
INNKEEPER:	Ho, ho!

THE KNIGHTS: Ho, ho, ho!

INNKEEPER: Stop that bloody racket! What is it you'd be waking me up for at this bloody hour?

SIR PERFLUOUS: We come in search of lodgings, good Innkeeper.

INNKEEPER: Tough! I'm all filled up! I've got a convention of Hobbits! Try the Diggers!

SIR PERFLUOUS: Nay, Innkeeper. You force us to reveal our Sacred Mission. Know then that we are four true Knights of King Arthur, late of the Round Table. Now in quest of the Holy Goose!

INNKEEPER: Ha! Hey, Maud! I've got four freaks in tin out here on a Holy Goose Chase! Sorry boys — no Goose here. But we've got a lot of snipe out back. I hear the grunion are running...

THE KNIGHTS: Come on...mount up...

FESTOON: (SINGS, TO "GREENSLEEVES")
We traveled many a hostile land,
The Sorghum Sea, the Burning Sand,
Past birds and bees and henbane trees,
And the Big Rock Candy Mountain.
At last we came to a forest's edge,
Surrounded by a boundless hedge,
And try as we might to form a wedge,
We could not pierce its thickness...
Gee, I'm running out of songs — we've been here a week!

SIR RAGLIO: I'm running out of henbane!

SIR PERFLUOUS: I'm running out of my iambic feet!

SOUND OF TERRIBLE SNAPPING

SIR VILE: Quiet! Snap dragons! Follow me, men. Look, there are their tracks! The dragons must have found a way in and out of the forest! Ready your lances! Chaaaaarrrgeeee!

THE KNIGHTS: Ha, ha! Ho, ho! Alarums!...

SOUND OF TERRIFIED BAA-ING

SHEPHERD: Boys! Boys! What are you doing? Stop! Those aren't dragons! Oh, my sheep, my lovely sheep! Have mercy! They are my sons, transformed into sheep by a Wicked Witch! Most of them are the Rightful Kings of Thessaly. Except for that one — he's a kingaroo.

SIR RAGLIO: Oh, Sir Vile! What have you done? Those aren't dragons!

SIR VILE: Well, they're kind of dragons...

FESTOON: (SINGING) Kind of a dragon, when the sheep get in your way...

SIR RAGLIO: Very nice, fool.

FESTOON: I'll write it down, and give it to my Lords Buckingham!

SHEPHERD: What are you knights? And what brings you to this wood to slaughter up my sons?

SIR VILE: This rotten map! Old Shepherd, are we anywhere near French Somaliland?

SHEPHERD: Ah! French Somaliland...

SIR VILE: German Togoland?... Dutch Wonderland?... British Honduras?...

SHEPHERD: I was foretold in a vision that four knights in search of the Holy Goose would come to me from Poland...

SIR RAGLIO: We didn't come from Poland...

SIR VILE: Shhhhhh!

SHEPHERD: So, boys, I'll just roast up one of my sons, and we can discuss this further...

THE KNIGHTS: He must know something! Right!

SHEPHERD: ...According to my vision, I have been given the power to reveal to you the several tasks you must perform in order to attain the requisite purity needed to capture the Holy goose. Look into my eyes, Sir Vile. What do you see?

SIR VILE: They're closed.

SHEPHERD: Sorry, I was counting my sons. Now look.

SIR VILE: You're sanpaku.

SHEPHERD: Look deeper!

SIR VILE: I can see for miles and miles and miles. I see a bravely appointed knight confronting, in single battle, a host of hopped-up hipping mad Harrison Saracics, and their dragons! And slickerty-slack and slick and blood and... He's through! He's smashed through an entire company of picaroons and he's dropped into a pool of molten lava and broken glass and sand fleas, and I can see his face — his poor tormented face — and it's the face of...me! Aaaaaaaugh...

SHEPHERD: Sir Raglio! It's your turn now. Look into my eyes. What do you see?

SIR RAGLIO: Hey! You have really beautiful eyes!

SHEPHERD: Look deeper!

SIR RAGLIO: It's her! I see her for the first time. It's Rita! She's walking towards me, out of the tower. She's just as beautiful as I thought. Oh, Rita, Rita! Now she's running to me in slow motion, her hair streaming out behind her. She looks a little like a military man. Now she's taking off her boiling-oil-soaked gown. She's standing in front of me, glorious in her innocent nakedness. She's radiant! She's ravishing! She's being ravished by a gibbering dwarf! Now she's being gibbered by a ravishing dwarf! Now she's being...oh, I can't look...

SIR PERFLUOUS:	Back, boy! I shall defend thee from thy fearful vision! Upon myself I'll take this loathsome sight!
FESTOON:	Let me see!
SHEPHERD:	No — Sir Perfluous, for you this test is meant...
SIR PERFLUOUS:	'Sblood! I see myself before the assembled courts of the world, in an amphitheater of vast, heroic size. I'm reading from the ninth volume of my Collected Memoirs. I turn the page to say what further deeds of greatness I have done, and to describe for them my single-handed battle with half-an-hundred Vandals who were wont to steal the kneecaps off my horse! But — awful! The crowned heads are laughing and reviling me! No! It is too much! I cannot watch!
SHEPHERD:	And now, Fool. Look you into my eyes. But stay downwind, will you? Look deeply, and tell me what you see.
FESTOON:	(SINGING) Iris, Iris Fancy Foods...
SHEPHERD:	No, Fool! Deeper! What do you see?
FESTOON:	I see your eyes. They're seeing me. What do you see?
SHEPHERD:	Ah! I spy the lies in eyes that hide the verity I see. The mirrored truth from you to me... What am I saying?
FESTOON:	Not bad. I think I'll write that down...
SHEPHERD:	Well, boys. Now that you have seen the tasks that lie before you, do you think they're worth it for the Holy Goose?
SIR RAGLIO:	Gee, sure they are! After all we've heard about this Holy Creature, it's worth any sacrifice! Why, its eyes are made of...of...say, what are its eyes made of?
SIR VILE:	I know not. But I have heard its feathers are of the finest...the finest...the purest...gems...eh, opals... What does it look like, old man?

SHEPHERD: Well, I happen to have an 8 by 10 glossy here in my wallet, along with some cheese...

SIR VILE: You have seen the fabled bird?

SHEPHERD: Many times. Look upon this picture.

SIR RAGLIO: Why, it's...it's...it's a goose...

SIR PERFLUOUS: Its...feathers are as white as — as — goose feathers...

SIR VILE: It looks exactly like a dragon I slew last month in Wessex.

FESTOON: (SINGING) Go tell Aunt Rhody, go tell Aunt Rhody...

SIR RAGLIO: But, wait a minute, guys! It must be special. Does it lay golden eggs?

SHEPHERD: No, it's just a plain, simple, run of the mill goose.

SIR VILE: Then, old man, why are we put to these terrible tests in order to capture it and bring it back to King Arthur?

SHEPHERD: My noble Lords. You, as True Knights of the Round Table should know best of all that "The value of the doing lies within the quest — not in the prize."

SIR RAGLIO: Guys, you know — he's right.

SIR VILE: I remember reading similar sentiments in the Poor Armorer's Almanack.[1]

---

1 In an abridged version of the script, the play ends here with this alternate dialogue:

SIR VILE: I remember reading similar sentiments in the Poor Armorer's Almanack.

SIR RAGLIO: You can't fight city hall...

SHEPHERD: Are you ready for to undertake your painful trials?

SIR VILE: We'll have to conference on that, shepherd... (THEY MULL IT OVER — AD LIB)

SIR PERFLUOUS: Our knightly Oath proclaims our duty plain!
To shirk it, we'd regret it.
About that Holy Goose that's naught but goose
Let's mount our steeds and get it!

SIR RAGLIO: But our horses were scared away by the snap dragons.

SIR VILE: Old shepherd, will you lend us a few of your sons?

SHEPHERD: Of course. They make wonderful steeds. Take those four. No, not that one! He's the kingaroo! Goodbye, lads.

THE KNIGHTS: (SINGING) High ho, high ho! It's after the Goose we go...

SHEPHERD: Ha! They've gone! Now, out of this silly disguise. Oof! There's cheese all over my wallet!

ARTHUR (DISGUISED AS A KINGAROO SHEEP) Baaaaaa!

MERLIN (FORMERLY DISGUISED AS A SHEPHERD) Ah! Arthur! Which one are you, boy? Oh, there you are — wearing your teeny, weeny crown. Poof!

ARTHUR: Oh, Merlin, heavy lies the head that wears the teeny weeny crown!

MERLIN: Well, that's the last of them. They've passed the test and gone. That noxious weed of henbane will never raise its flowery head within the circled court of Table Round. Or something like it.

SIR RAGLIO: As knights, we know our duty plain...
SIR VILE: To shirk it, we'd regret it...
SIR PERFLUOUS: And thanks to you, the path is clear...
FESTOON: About that goose —
ALL: FORGET IT!

ALL SING — AD LIB

ANNOUNCER: And so, you've heard the Firesign Theatre's retelling of the true story of THE SWORD AND THE STONED. This tale has come down as legend through many authors, and is now available to the general public as a beautiful musical film — "The Pawnbroker".

ARTHUR: Merlin, my faithful councilor...

MERLIN: Yes, sire?

ARTHUR: Before we return to the pomp and circumstance of our court, to set aright the sinking garden of state, o'ergrown with thornéd barnacles all rank and gross, would you do me a little, little favor?

MERLIN: A teeny, weeny favor?

ARTHUR: Yes. There was some business I was about, whilst in the guise of playful sheep, that needs must taken care of be.

MERLIN: What?

ARTHUR: I must nibble further of yonder herb. The juice of which on sleeping pallet laid will dispel the evil humors which have arisen late in my troubled soul.

MERLIN: But, Arthur! What you've been nibbling at...

ARTHUR: That's an order, you doting sorcerer!

MERLIN: Very well, my lord. Poof!

ARTHUR: Baaaa! Baaaa! Chomp, chomp...

MERLIN: Oh, piteous time! Oh, wanton age! My sorcerer's heart it heaves — to see my noble Arthur there, consuming henbane leaves...

THE KNIGHTS: (SINGING) Hey nonny, nonny...

ANNOUNCER: The Firesign Theatre has just presented THE SWORD AND THE STONED — a Romantic Legend of Olden Tymes. And so good night unto you all. Give us your hands, if we be friends...

MUSIC THEME FADES UP

SESAME MUCHO

Performed live at the Magic Mushroon and broadcast on KRLA-AM on December 10, 1967.

ORIGINAL CAST

Phil Austin as Artunian, Old Man 3

Peter Bergman as Announcer, Fred, Captain Salt, Thief, Old Wazoo, Old Man 2

David Ossman as Major, Pasha, Old Man 4

Phil Proctor as Tabu, Old Man 1, Admiral

SESAME MUCHO

ANNOUNCER: The Firesign Theatre presents a golden hit from the thirties...

VOICE: (PUFF) It's gold!

VOICE: Eureka!

VOICE: You don't smell bad yourself!

ANNOUNCER: ...the immortal SESAME MUCHO.

VOICE: (SINGING, AS IF ON A SCRATCHED 78 RECORD) "Sesame, Sesame Mucho...da da da da da da da da da, da da da da da... Sesame (TICK) Sesame (TICK) Sesame (TICK) Sesame (TICK)..."

MAJOR: Take that record off the turntable, Tabu. It sticks.

TABU: Yes, Sahib Major.

MAJOR: Thank you. Now, the Royal All-Peoples Neogeophysical Amateur Explorers Club, Den 14...

TABU: 15, Sahib.

MAJOR: 15. Thank you, Tabu - will come to order (VOICES INTERRUPT: HERE HERE!) What you have just heard was the last recorded words of Admiral Beard and his All Husky Orchestra, somewhat delayed by the Christmas Island mails. (HERE HERE!) Although we've just received it, the package is dated 1934...

TABU: 5, Sahib.

MAJOR: 1534. Thank you, Tabu. (HERE HERE!) And, as the Admiral has not attended any of the weekly meetings of our beloved Society (HERE HERE!) since that time — a period of 34 years...

TABU: 5, Sahib.

MAJOR: 54 years, thank you Bamboo. You're on your toes.

TABU: No, you're on my toes, Major.

MAJOR: As he has not attended 3,354 meetings...

TABU: Very good, Sahib.

MAJOR: Thank you. We shall have to mark him tardy. (HERE HERE)

TABU: Mmmmmmmmmmmm.

MAJOR: On that somber note, let me have my faceless Indian houseboat, Kazoo, call the roll.

TABU: (CLEARS THROAT) Sweet roll? Not here. Jelly roll? Not here. Rock'n...

MAJOR: No, not those rolls...

TABU: Oh, I'm sorry. Royce...

MAJOR: No, not the car either! Let me do it. Me? Here. Everyone else?

VOICES (AS ON A BROKEN RECORD): Here here! (TICK) Here here! (TICK) Here here! (TICK) Here here! (TICK)...

MAJOR: No, I can't stand it! Turn off that gramophone, little Bamboo. The sweet voices of our last fully attended convention cannot fill the void created by this sea of empty chairs floating before my eyes. Oh, Banana, I'm so lonely! Where have all the Fellows gone?

TABU:	Long time, isn't it. Don't worry sir — they'll each one of them be back, someday, surely.
MAJOR:	My name's not Shirley. Call me Major, Tabu.
TABU:	All right, Major Tabu. Don't worry your old grey foot, sir.
MAJOR:	It ain't what it used to be, is it?
TABU:	They will return soon from their expeditions and bring back untold riches from the lost treasure cave of El Seed.
MAJOR:	I told you not to untold that.
TABU:	I'm unworthy, Sahib.
MAJOR:	No, Rattan! It's all over! They're lost, and I'm too old, and too gout-ridden, and too basically disinterested to go look for them. What we need is some fresh blood.
TABU:	Well, I've got an ailing baby elephant and some leeches in the kitchen, Sahib. I'll be right back. Just hold on.
MAJOR:	If you say so.
TABU:	No! Let go, sir!
MAJOR:	Oh, sorry.
TABU:	Sahib, I'll see you later.
MAJOR:	No, my name is Shirley.
TABU:	(OFF) I'm sorry!
MAJOR:	Oh, you don't understand! Oh, how can I recruit some new members?
SOUND:	KNOCK KNOCK
MAJOR:	Too obvious, but come in anyway.

SOUND: DOOR

ARTUNIAN: I'd like to join the Club and get my maps. Are you the man I'm supposed to see?

MAJOR: Oh, young man! I'm so happy to see you. Pull up an elephant foot and sit down.

ARTUNIAN: Thank you.

MAJOR: Ow! No, not that one, that's my foot! I have the gout, you know. Just turn over this umbrella stand, sit down and fill out this form.

ARTUNIAN: (WHISTLE) Whatta tomato! This form is filled out already! Now can I get my maps?

MAJOR: Of course. Just as soon as you sign this tomato.

ARTUNIAN: Good. I'm trying to get to Oxnard before they clean it.

TABU: Here you are, Sahib. I'm sorry —

MAJOR: No, you're Tabu!

TABU: ...the elephants were all drained dry by the leeches, the hungry little devils. I didn't realize they were all day suckers.

ARTUNIAN: This pen is out of ink.

MAJOR: That's no problem. Dip it in a little leech blood.

ARTUNIAN: But it's a ball point.

TABU: Then have a leechee nut.

MAJOR: Ah! He's signed! Our first new member in 40 years.

TABU: 5, Sahib.

MAJOR: 5 years.

TABU: 45 years, Sahib.

MAJOR: 45 years.

TABU: No, that's not right either. Oh, well...say whatever you want.

ARTUNIAN: Now can I have my maps?

MAJOR: Of course. Tabu, get this young man a selection of maps.

TABU: (OFF) Yes Sahib!

ARTUNIAN: Gee, I'm glad I finally joined the Club. I've got a couple of weeks of vacation coming, and I don't have to pick up my unemployment check until Thursday afternoon, and so I'll be doing a lot of traveling, and you never know with an old wreck like mine when you'll need a tow, or a flat changed. Can you recommend a scenic route to Oxnard?

TABU: Here are your maps, Sahib.

MAJOR: Oxnard, you say? Well, I was there in ought 14...but there's nothing of interest there, except for the Mounds, and they've been cleaned. So I don't know what you'd want to go there for...

TABU: Five...

MAJOR: I don't know what you'd want to go there five. However, would you be interested in my recommendation?

ARTUNIAN: Yes, of course. That's why I joined the Club.

MAJOR: Then I would suggest that you, like all our other members, pay a visit to the Treasure Cave of El Seed.

ARTUNIAN: Fine. Where is it?

MAJOR: We aren't quite sure, but here's a map which will help you.

ARTUNIAN: I don't see any map.

MAJOR: It's tattooed on Rangoon's back. Take off your shirt, boy.

SOUND: RIPPPPP

ARTUNIAN: Oh, it's a strip map.

MAJOR: Yes. It will enable you to follow in the footsteps of the other Club members. See, this is the Club Foot here. Slip it on and Fred will dance you to the door.

ARTUNIAN: Fred?

MAJOR: Yes, Fred — our dancing bear.

ARTUNIAN: Fred? A bear?

MAJOR: Yes, Fred Abear.

SOUND: TAP DANCE ROUTINE

FRED: Hi! Fred Abear, your dancing master, here. My train just broke down in this little town, which must mean there's a member of the local High School basketball team who's dying — unless I throw a benefit for him.

MAJOR: Fred, we have a new member. Show him the steps.

FRED: Now, young man — gotcha Club Foot on? Fine! This is the Arthur Murray Magic Step. Careful now — you're leading. And these are the Russian Steps.

ARTUNIAN: Who's that at the top?

FRED: Zhivago. He's the Doc at the top of the steppes.

SOUND: ANIMAL GROWL

FRED: Careful! That's the Steppenwolf. Whoops! Would you please pick up my handkerchief?

ARTUNIAN: Yes, here.

FRED: Thank you. You've just done the Stepinfetchit!

MAJOR: Why don't you show him the door?

FRED: Let's jam a little.

ARTUNIAN: Oh — we're doing the door jam.

FRED: No, it's the door step!

ARTUNIAN: Well, I'm off for my two-week vacation at the Treasure Cave of El Seed.

MAJOR: Don't forget your map! Go with him, too, Tattoo.

TABU: Three, Tatthree, Sahib.

MAJOR: Get out! And take this precious record of Admiral Beard singing "Sesame Mucho", which is our only clue to the actual whereabouts of the Cave.

ARTUNIAN: This old door won't open.

TABU: Then — rapidly — through the transom, sir.

ARTUNIAN: Oh! You have rapid transom here. (SQUEEZES)

TABU: All right now — come with me. I'm sorry to leave the old Major, but he's gotten gout, so I'm getting gout, too, me.

ARTUNIAN: It sure is nice of the Club to give me an Indian guide.

TABU: It's better than having your guide give you an Indian Club... (CLUB) Well, it's just that I've got this map on my back, and it's driving me to distraction. Would you mind? It's just down the block.

ARTUNIAN: No. We can take my balloon. It's parked over here, on this lamp post.

TABU: What an unusual way of traveling. How did you come by it?

ARTUNIAN: Free, from Ralph Williams. No balloon payments. Shimmy up the post and get in.

TABU: Oh goodness gracious, I don't have to do that. Ha ha! I can perform the Indian Rope Trick for you.

ARTUNIAN: I've heard about that. Can I see it?

TABU: You can do it yourself. Let me give you a helping hemp. Drag on this rope.

ARTUNIAN: (DRAGS)

TABU: Here we go up, higher and higher, into the balloon.

CAPT. SALT: Welcome aboard, har har har.

TABU: Goody gracious Sahib! Who's that old sailor with the peg leg?

SALT: I be Captain Salt of the Istanballoon Express.

TABU: Then why are you dressed in a severe black suit and vibrating?

ARTUNIAN: Captain Salt is a Shaker.

TABU: But look! He's wearing that ornate crucifix.

SALT: I've always been attracted by the opposite sect, haresy haresy haresy.

ARTUNIAN: Let's cut that line.

SALT: If you say so. There! We're off. Drop some ballast!

SOUND: BALLAST DROPS — WOMAN YELPS

SALT: You flattened that poor old lady down there!

ARTUNIAN: Which one?

TABU: The one in the ballast blue gown! But we're still falling, Captain!

SALT:	Oh! I remember! The balloon's upside down! I parked it that way in case of rain.
TABU:	Good thinking, Captain. Let's just turn it right side up.
SALT:	Heave har, me ho hos!
SOUND:	BALLOON RIGHTED — SLIDE WHISTLE
SALT:	Here we go! Check the wind!
SOUND:	WIND
SALT:	Thar she blows! It's a North Wind.
SOUND:	WIND AND COUGH
SALT:	It's an ill wind.
SOUND:	INTAKE OF WIND
SALT:	Ah, good! It's a head wind!
ARTUNIAN:	We're off to find the Treasure Cave of El Seed!
SALT:	Check the map first!
ARTUNIAN:	Bend over, Tabu. I want to find the Antelope Valley Freeway. Yes! Captain, see here? It runs just over these foothills.
SALT:	Foothills? Then we're off course.
ARTUNIAN:	Off course?
SALT:	Of course! Hard to starboard!
ARTUNIAN:	It sure is!
TABU:	Wait! What foothills are you talking about? There are no foothills on my map!

ARTUNIAN:	Off course there are. Right by your shoulder blade...
TABU:	Those aren't foothills, those are goosebumps, you bunny!
SALT:	Then we're lost! And there's a storm brewing...
TABU:	Two lumps, please!
SALT:	No time! Hold on! We're falling! We're in a terrible downdraft! Burn your downdraft card!
ARTUNIAN:	No, no! The balloon is flammable. We'd go up in smoke!
TABU:	We've got to go up somehow.
SALT:	We've got to rise above this storm.
TABU:	Think nice thoughts.
SALT:	Wait! There's some emergency ballast in that box the dealer threw in. Open it and throw it out.
SOUND:	BOX OPENING
RALPH:	Hi, friends. Ralph Williams, owner and operator of Ralph Williams Balloon, here at the largest...
SALT (OVER):	Throw him off!
ARTUNIAN:	It's not enough!
SALT:	Throw everything over!
ARTUNIAN:	I'll throw over my watch.
TABU:	I'll throw over my lunch.
ARTUNIAN:	I'll throw over my wallet.
TABU:	I'll throw over my government.

SALT:	Anything else?
TABU:	All I have left is this funny cigarette. I hate to do it, but here it goes.
SALT:	Don't do that!
TABU:	I've done it.
SALT:	Then we're a cigarette lighter!
SOUND:	FLAMES
ARTUNIAN:	We're going to crash!
TABU:	And about time, too. I'm exhausted!
ARTUNIAN:	Hold on!
SOUND:	CRASH, SCREAMS
ARTUNIAN:	Where are we, Captain?
SALT:	Here.
ARTUNIAN:	Thank goodness! I thought we were lost.
SALT:	Don't worry. As soon as I can spot a familiar cloud and fix the balloon, we'll be on our way.
TABU:	But we lost our way during the storm, along with my lunch.
ARTUNIAN:	We may have lost our way, but we haven't lost our Kurds. Here comes a band of them now.
WHISTLING:	STARS AND STRIPES FOREVER
SALT:	That's not a band of Kurds, that's a band of thieves.
ARTUNIAN:	Are they for us or against us? Which side are they on?
SALT:	It doesn't look good, lads! They're band 4, side 2!

RECORD:	BOB DYLAN "SUBTERRANEAN HOMESICK BLUES"
ARTUNIAN:	That's not a bad band, Zazu...
TABU:	I don't know. I find it a cut below band 3, side 2 myself.
SOUND:	WHISTLE
ARTUNIAN:	That's their leader?
VOICE:	(SINGS) Ich liebe der vogel in der sonne mich, Ich liebe der vogel und ich liebe dich.
SALT:	He's only the German lieder. Here's the man in charge.
PASHA:	Well, boys — who do we have here?
ARTUNIAN:	Us.
PASHA:	I thought so. What am I going to do with Us?
SALT:	That's your problem.
PASHA:	So it is. Let me introduce myself. (AD LIB) I'm Sir Robin Pasha, leader of this band of 40 thieves.
TABU:	39, Sahib.
PASHA:	Counting myself — 40.
TABU:	I'm sorry!
PASHA:	You must be the three men in a gasbag about which we have heard so little, here in the land of burning sands.
THIEF:	Oh, the sand *is* burning, Great Pasha.
PASHA:	Call the fire department.
THIEF:	Here they come now — carrying buckets of fire.

PASHA:	Good! They're fighting fire with fire.
ARTUNIAN:	What did you say about us being the three men in a gasbag about which you had heard so little?
PASHA:	Did I say that?
ARTUNIAN:	Yes.
PASHA:	Well, you just said it, too.
TABU:	Three, Sahib.
ARTUNIAN:	What?
PETER:	What?
TABU:	Oh, never mind.
PASHA:	You three men have arrived at a very opportune moment — just in time to fulfill a great prophecy. Start with that one. You'll find the shovels in the corner.
THIEF:	(IN DISTANCE) Hala in haboot ma al ben ikmir!
TABU:	What's that Chinese bandit on the sand dune so excited about?
PASHA:	Shhh! According to that scout, fair game for our merry band of thieves is coming near. Quick! Behind that rock!
SOUND:	SCRAMBLING
ARTUNIAN:	Gee, isn't this exciting? Romantic Arabian thieves ready to rob something! Maybe a caravan filled with gold, incense and peppermints!
TABU:	Not to mention camel droppings.
ARTUNIAN:	Don't mention that!

TABU: I'm sorry.

BEGGAR: (WHISTLES "WHENEVER I'M AFRAID")

TABU: Why, it's only a poor old blind beggar...

PASHA: Charge!

SOUND: TERRIFIC BATTLE

PASHA: Excellent, men! We've won the battle. (HUZZAH) Bring me the spoils.

THIEF: Don't you want the fresh stuff?

PASHA: All right! What did we get?

THIEF: Two dates, a loincloth and a beggar's bowl. (HUZZAH)

PASHA: Is that all the old man had?

TABU: He had fleas too, I see!

PASHA: Aha! Robin Pasha and his 40 thieves have done it again. We robbed the poor to give to the poor. Us. Off to the Citadel!

SALT: Aye, but what about me balloon?

PASHA: Don't look back, Captain Salt.

SALT: Why?

PASHA: Because you'll turn into a pillar of man. Saddle the camels, men! Forward camels!

VOICE: (OFF) Forward camels!

ARTUNIAN: Why are we walking?

PASHA: We have to walk a mile for our camels.

SOUND: ARABIAN MUSIC (ISKADARA) WITH TAMBOURINE

VOICES: Onward! Forward ho!

TABU: I know that song: “Raga Around the Clock”.

PASHA: I like that song, Tabu. Would you sing it again if I gave you a camel?

TABU: For a camel — certainly, Pasha. (SINGS) 1 — 2 — 3 — 4 — 5 — Begin. (AD LIB)

PASHA: You sing very well for a camel. Where did you learn?

TABU: I was in a band in my hometown, Pasha.

PASHA: Where was that?

TABU: Gary, India! I played with Ali Sander’s Raga Time Band. (SINGS, TO “76 TROMBONES”) “76 sitars led the big parade, with 110 tambura close behind...”

PASHA: Wonderful! More wine! More food! Bring in the other date!

TABU: What?

SALT: We appreciate your hospitality, Pasha, but I can’t help noticing that for robbers you seem to live a very frugal life.

PASHA: That is true. And therein lies a tale.

TABU: I’m sorry, I must have dropped it.

PASHA: I am the third...

TABU: Fourth, Sahib.

PASHA: Third!

TABU: You’re welcome!

PASHA: Descendant in a direct line from the greatest thief in the history of Arabia...or a Rabia. The legendary El Seed. He robbed this country blind — had he had his eyesight, it would have been even worse.

ARTUNIAN: But what did he do with his booty?

PASHA: He bronzed it and hung it on his camel. When it got too heavy, he kept it hidden with all his other treasure, in an immense cave, to which only he knew the combination. On his deathbed he passed on to me the words which would open the door from the outside. But he died before he could tell me the secret of how to open the door from the inside.

ARTUNIAN: Why, then — that must be the famous Treasure Cave of El Seed! Oh, let's go see it! How do you get in?

TABU: What is it you say?

SALT: I suppose it's something from a fairy tale — like "open sesame".

SOUND: DOORS OPENING

PASHA: Don't say that! Those words not only open the door to the Treasure Cave, but they also open every door in the Citadel. And it's drafty.

SOUND: DOORS CLOSING

ARTUNIAN: But all the doors are closed again.

TABU: Oh, and there's a problem. If we go into the Cave, we'll never get out again.

PASHA: You would not, Tabu. But your friend might.

ARTUNIAN: Who? Me? Why?

PASHA: Because of the prophecy that our Court Dervish, the Exalted Old Wazoo, came up with after smoking the last of our sesame seeds. I'll call him in with this

	ancient Persian incantation, so that he may tell you himself. (CHANTS) How's your mother — how's your brother — how's your Sister Sue? And while we're on the subject — here's the Old Wazooooo.
SOUND:	CYMBAL CRASH
WAZOO:	You called? Hello there. I, as you may have guessed, am the Old Wazoo. I was not always called so. In my youth I was known as the Young Wazoo. Would you like to hear the prophecy?
PASHA:	Not particularly.
ARTUNIAN:	I would. I think it has something to do with me.
WAZOO:	Well, here goes! (SINGS IN "ARABIC")
ARTUNIAN:	What's that in English?
WAZOO:	A white man will come to come in, and, although he be left, it is right that he go back to come out.
ARTUNIAN:	What does that mean?
WAZOO:	I don't have the foggiest.
TABU:	I'm sorry, I had it right here, I must have dropped it...
WAZOO:	But I wish someone would figure it out. I haven't had a good smoke of sesame in years. I used to be the High Exalted Grand Old Wazoo — but not anymore!
PASHA:	There you have it, young man.
WAZOO:	Oh, he's got it. Give it back to me.
ARTUNIAN:	I do? What is it?
PASHA:	It's our only chance. Will you enter the cave, fulfill the prophecy, bring wealth and prosperity back to our country, so that we can once again steal from the rich and give to the rich?

ARTUNIAN: Yes.

PASHA: Knowing full well that you may be locked forever in eternal darkness?

ARTUNIAN: No!

SALT: Well, in that case, there's nothing more to keep us here. Let's get back to the balloon and look for the Antelope Freeway.

PASHA: You mean you're going to leave us destitute?

TABU: Yes.

PASHA: After we have wined you, and dined you on our last two dates in Arabia?

ARTUNIAN: Oh? Where do you play next?

TABU: No, Sahib. What the Pasha means to say is that it is a tradition in all countries in the Eastern part of the world to give thanks for the meal you have just enjoyed by expressing one's delight at the hospitality proffered, in an act of entertainment or similar feats of valor. It is the least that we could do to sing a little something for him, and make our escape during the last three bars.

ARTUNIAN: But I don't know how to sing. And I can't even remember the Arthur Murray Magic Step. What shall we do?

SALT: Why don't you juggle this record?

TABU: Oh, no, Sahib! That's a wonderful idea. We can play the record for him. Here, I'll wind up the gramophone...

VOICE: Oooo! Stop that, sonny!

TABU: Sorry, Gramma. Here it goes...

SOUND: RECORD PLAYS "SESAME MUCHO"

PASHA:	Why, I'd recognize that scratch anywhere. That's the voice of Admiral Beard!
TABU:	Where did you hear of Admiral Beard?
PASHA:	He was the last of those damned amateur explorers who all managed to get themselves trapped inside the Treasure Cave.
TABU:	What did you say!? Those must be all the missing members of our Club!
ARTUNIAN:	Our Club?
TABU:	Yes.
ARTUNIAN:	They are?
TABU:	Yes.
ARTUNIAN:	Then it's my duty to go in and get them out. Where is the Cave?
PASHA:	Right this way. There it is.
SALT:	That great immovable stone?
PASHA:	No, that's the Old Wazoo! He must have gotten hold of some sesame seeds. Ignore him. Now — entering the Cave is a very dangerous and difficult operation. You have to be very careful how and where you stand, because you'll have very little time after I say "open sesame"...
SOUND:	DOOR OPENING
PASHA:	Oops! I said it! In you go — goodbye and good luck!
SOUND:	DOOR SLAM
ARTUNIAN:	Gee, it sure is dark in here. Well, I guess I might as well start trying. Open Sesame! Nothing. They were right!

OLD MAN 1: Of course they were.

ARTUNIAN: Who's that?

OLD MAN 1: Pull up a bag of sesame seeds and sit down. We'll have a report from you later.

ARTUNIAN: Why, you must be the lost explorers!

OLD MAN 2: Don't rub it in. Get on with it, Fred.

OLD MAN 1: The 3355th consecutive meeting of the Royal All-Peoples Neogeophysical Explorer's Club, Den 14, In Exile, will come to order. Wherever you are. I wish we could get some lights in here.

OLD MAN 2: Burn some more sesame seeds. (HERE HERE)

OLD MAN 3: No, no! The last time we did that, we were stoned for weeks!

OLD MAN 4: Three weeks!

OLD MAN 2: Two! Two weeks. I remember.

OLD MAN 3: I'm still out.

OLD MAN 4: If anyone calls, I'm out too.

OLD MAN 2: You're out three.

OLD MAN 1: Three outs! Who's up?

OLD MAN 3: We're all up! (HERE HERE)

OLD MAN 1: Gentlemen! Gentlemen, please! Let's hear the report of the Emergency Escape Committee. Have they found a way out?

OLD MAN 2: Apparently so. They're not here.

OLD MAN 3 (SARTRE): Yes we are! We're over here under this pile of treasure.

OLD MAN 1: All right, then, Professor Sartre. Give us your report on the escape possibilities from Cave 14-dash-B.

OLD MAN 3 (SARTRE): No exit. (ICI! ICI!)

OLD MAN 1: Then we're still trapped. (MUMBLING) Let's conclude this meeting, as we have all those in the past, with our beloved Club Anthem, sung by Admiral you-know-who.

ADMIRAL: Sesame, sesame mucho... No! I can't do it! I've forgotten the words in the dark! (MUMBLING)

ARTUNIAN: Hey! Don't worry! I've got a recording of your anthem right here!

OLD MAN 3: Who said that?

OLD MAN 2: Gentlemen, how wonderful! We're having another mass hallucination.

ARTUNIAN: No, I'm very real. And I can help the Admiral, because I've got his original recording, and I'll play it for you on Tabu's portable gramophone. Now, how do I wind this up...?

OLD MAN 1: Gentlemen, what a pleasant surprise. The entertainment committee has arranged for a musical treat. (COUGHS) Are you ready, young man?

ARTUNIAN: Yeah, well — this is a right-handed machine, and I'm left-handed... Could you turn the cave around?

OLD MAN 3: Just play it!

SOUND: RECORD PLAYS BACKWARDS — "OHCUM EMASES, EMASES"

SOUND: CAVE DOOR OPENS

OLD MEN: We're free! Run for it! Grab everything you can! Hurry!

SOUND: CAVE DOOR CLOSES — HEAVY BREATHING

PASHA: You've done it, young man! How did you discover the secret? What is it?

ARTUNIAN: It was simple. All I did was wind Tabu's gramophone backwards and play this broken record... Oh! It must have gotten broken in the rush...

PASHA: Then we're lost! There's nothing left in Arabia worth stealing. It's locked up forever. What are we to do now?

SALT: Say, look at all those old men. They brought out enough sesame seeds to stay stoned for a month!

TABU: Sahib Pasha! Could you not plant those seeds?

PASHA: Yes, I could not. But my men could.

ARTUNIAN: Then you can give up your life of crime, and enjoy the benefits of an agrarian peace!

TABU: The country will become prosperous!

SALT: Trade will flourish!

PASHA: Then I can steal it all back again!

TABU: Then you'll give up your wicked ways?

ARTUNIAN: Do you concede?

SALT: You can seed the country!

ARTUNIAN: Oh, say you can seed!

PASHA: By the dawn's early light — I *can* seed! For miles, and miles, and miles...

RECORD: DEVIL'S ANVIL "WALA DAI"

ANNOUNCER: The Firesign Theatre has presented SESAME MUCHO — a tale of adventure and intrigue, in Persia, in English, In Shallah, with Italian subtitles!

The Armenian's Paw

Performed live at the Magic Mushroom and broadcast on KRLA-AM on December 17, 1967.

ORIGINAL CAST

Phil Austin as Harry, Telegram Boy, Old Man

Peter Bergman as Dr. Firesign

David Ossman as Announcer, Mr. Archer

Philip Proctor as Leo, Lama

The Armenian's Paw

MUSIC:	THEME IN AND UNDER
ANNOUNCER:	The Firesign Theatre Presents: THE ARMENIAN'S PAW, or: BUFFALO CHIPS WON'T YOU COME OUT TONIGHT, or: THE ARMENIAN'S PAW, or: NONE OF THE ABOVE...

MUSIC UP AND OUT

ANN:	The Scene: The faded grandeur of the Teatro Burrito Grande Theater in downtown Guacamole, Chile...
VOICE:	And I'll have the number three dinner, please, dear.
ANN:	...where at this very moment, in the flickering lime-light of the gas-lit stage...
OTHER VOICE:	Hold the refried beans on mine, please.
ANN:	...Dr. Firesign's Original Traveling Antique Theatre of the Plains and Buffalo Show is concluding the 8,412th continuous performance of its immortal favorite...Waiting for the Count of Monte Cristo, or Someone Like Him.

CROSS TO THEATRE

ARCHER:	...And so you, Edmond Dantes, are the true Count of Monte Cristo!
HARRY:	I am?

ARCHER: No, you're not!

DR FIRESIGN: Because I am!

HARRY: But that's impossible!

LEO: How's that?

DR. F: Fine, thanks. How's this?

LEO: Not bad.

ARCHER: Not good!

HARRY: Why not?

LEO: Because you are my sister!

DR. F: Then we can never be married!

ARCHER: I knew it all along.

HARRY: But we *are* married!

LEO: So are we!

HARRY: Thank god! (DIES)

ARCHER: Our friend the Count of...um...

DR. F: (WHISPERS) Monte Christo!

ARCHER: Monte Cristo. Our friend the Count of Monte Christo is dead. And so, with saddened heart and lowered head, let's leave the gentlemen in peace. Dead, the feast.

ALL: Er, to the feast. To the feast.

CROWD: Boo! What a bummer? Go home bum! Do any of you know "I Am a Walrus"? Show us your buffalo! Terrible! RAZZ Etc.

DR. F:	Gentlemen — we're very pleased that you should ask for our buffalo. Our troupe would like to thank you for the one and a half beautiful days that we've spent in Guacamole.
VOICE:	Go home!
DR. F:	Here's a token of our appreciation. Catch!
VOICE 2:	Hey man, this is a token for the IRC!
VOICE:	That's the best thing you've said all night! Up the Irish!
VOICE 2:	Hey man, you better shuffle out your buffalo.
DR. F:	Ladies and gentlemen! With your kind indulgence, please! Our performance tonight will conclude — as advertised — with Dr. Firesign's world-renowned Buffalo Tableau in Three Scenes...
VOICES:	WHISTLES AND APPLAUSE
HARRY:	The buffalo's sick, Doctor Firesign.
DR. F:	Well, the buffalo must go on!
HARRY:	But he just threw up all over my trunk!
DR. F:	I don't care.
HARRY:	I do! It's my trunk!
DR. F:	Well, it's my buffalo! And he's on!
SOUND:	DRUMROLL
DR. F:	Tableau One! "The American Buffalo At Play!"
SOUND:	CYMBAL CRASH
ART:	(GROANING) mrmrmrmrmrmrmr
SOUND:	DRUMROLL

DR. F: Tableau Two! "The American Buffalo Pursued By An American Indian!"

SOUND: CYMBAL CRASH

ART: mrmrmrmrmrmrmr

SOUND: DRUMROLL

DR. F: Tableau Three! "The Death of the American Buffalo!"

SOUND: CYMBAL CRASH

ART: mrmrmrmrmrmrmr — (COUGH)

SOUND: OMINOUS GRUMBLING

DR. F: Let's get out of here, boys!

ARCHER: Don't forget the buffalo!

DR F: I wish I could!

HARRY: Run for your lives...

DOOR SLAM FOLLOWED BY HEAVY BREATHING

DR. F: Lock the door. All right, are we all here?

LEO: Where's the buffalo?

HARRY: He's in the bathroom.

DR. F: Go hold his head, Harry.

HARRY: All right.

DR. F: Leo, start packing! Now that the buffalo's gone, we can talk.

LEO: I sure hope they don't find out which hotel we're staying at.

KNOCK KNOCK

ARCHER: It's too late! The same thing happened to me once in Springfield...

DR. F: Shhhh! Get the door, Leo.

DOOR OPENS

BOY: Hello! Is this the Firestone Antique Theater of the Plains?

DR. F: They just left.

BOY: Oh, that's too bad. I got a telegram for them.

ARCHER: Well, boy, they left their buffalo. You can give it to him.

ART: mrmrmrmrmrmrmr

BOY: Hey! That's a pretty nice buffalo for a '58, man. It's been lowered, huh? All right, stand back. You going to get a singing telegram! (SINGS, TO "HOW ARE THINGS IN GLOCCA MORRA")
"How are things in Guacamole?
Is my little troupe still playing there?
'Cause if they run you out of town,
Don't wear a frown!
You're booked in Yucatan!
Bat City. Two weeks. Lots a luck. Signed, your agent, Buffalo Billy Morris. P. S. Is the buffalo feeling any better?" You got a reply?

ART: mrmrmrmrmrmrmr

BOY: How do you spell mrmrmrmrmrmrmr?

DR. F: With a double mrmr! Get out!

DOOR SLAMS

ARCHER: Bat City, Yucatan! It's the end!

LEO: What's the matter with Bat City?

DR F: Bat City, my boy, is Act Six.

ARCHER: It's like playing for your parents.

LEO: But if we open in Bat City...

HARRY: Nobody opens in Bat City, lad. It's always closing night.

DR F: Well, gentlemen — what could we expect in an age when no one appreciates Art?

ART: mrmrmrmrmrmrmr

DR F: Quiet, Art! We're all in this together. Everybody put on a disguise, and we'll go out and have a drink at the Cantina.

TRANSITION SOUNDS — CAR HORNS, SPANISH VOICES

LEO: Well, maybe we could quit show business instead of playing Bat City.

ARCHER: It's the same thing, boy.

HARRY: There must be another town we can play.

LEO: We've run out of towns.

DR F: No, we've been run out of towns.

ARCHER: It's the same thing.

HARRY: Where's the Cantina? I'm thirsty.

ARCHER: It's over there on the corner.

HARRY: When are they going to put it in a building?

LEO: Where did Art go?

DR. F: He just shuffled into that little gift shop. He must be hunting for a souvenir.

ARCHER: Well, quick, get him! He hasn't any money!

HARRY: He has a couple of human nickels.

DR F: Follow him!

DING DING DINGLE DING

ARTUNIAN: Good evening, gentlemen. Welcome to Artunian's Lamentable Antique Store and Curio Hut.

HARRY: Excuse me, but we're looking for a buffalo.

ARTUNIAN: Curios you should mention that. The Shah of Persia only yesterday personally gave me this most exquisite beast. Look you - totally hand-encrusted with precious wool. As you can tell, it's been lowered. For a '58, it's a very clean machine. Would you like me to wrap it, or will you eat it here?

HARRY: Art! Art, it's you!

ART: mrmrmrmrmrmr

DR F: Take that hastily scrawled price-tag off his horns!

ARCHER: You ought to be ashamed of yourself, Mr. Artunian.

ARTUNIAN: Yes, I should. Why don't you putter around the shop while I put on my hair shirt. Be sure and look for the cleverly hidden Maps of various Lost Cities. And feel free to break some ashtrays, I need the money.

HARRY: Gee, what as strange man. Did you notice that when he put his right hand in his pocket — he didn't?

LEO: I wonder how he lost his hand?

ARCHER: Look, boys! A rare Egyptian Death's-head Moth in quartz.

LEO: For fifty dollars!

DR F: That's a bit much. I wonder if he has it in pints. But wait! Look! Over here. Do you see what I see, vaguely outlined through this imitation milk-glass copy of an Assyrian Middle Kingdom séance Toby Jug?

ALL: No!

DR F: Well, look closer. It's what appears to be a carefully rolled ancient map-sized papyrus. Is the Armenian still in the back?

ARTUNIAN: Yes, I'm still back here.

HARRY: I can't see hide nor hair shirt of him.

DR F: Then cover me.

ALL: OK!

DR F: No, boys! Get those rugs off me! Now see what you've done! My hand is caught inside the jug!

ARTUNIAN: Well! What a pleasant surprise! Your hand seems to be trapped inside my priceless Assyrian Toby Jug.

DR F: Why, so it is!

ARTUNIAN: Your hand is more important than any priceless jug. You see, I who have only one hand know the value of hands. Go ahead, smash it!

DR F: That's awfully good of you, Artunian.

LOUD CRASH

ARTUNIAN: Ah! You're free — and you owe me twenty dollars.

DR F: The money is of no importance. Take a look at this papyrus I found.

ARTUNIAN: The papyrus?

HARRY:	Gently, lads, it's been tied securely with Armenian string cheese.
DR F:	Let me see...Aha! It's an ancient Assyrian...price tag for twenty dollars!
ARTUNIAN:	Ah, how equitable.
HARRY:	Look, Dr. Firesign! On the back of the price tag is a...
DR F:	Why, isn't it a...
LEO:	Yes, it is!
HARRY:	No it isn't. It's an authentic map of a fabled lost city, surely filled with valuable relics and the elixir of eternal youth. Let's go find it!
ARTUNIAN:	Drat! I've been looking for that for years! To have been outwitted in this tragic way by simple tourists! Ooooooo!
DR F:	Sorry, old man. You'll have to make the best of a bad bargain.
HARRY:	While we make the best of this map. Can you decipher these strange occult symbols, Mr. Archer?
ARCHER:	Of course. Let me look. Mmmm...three Birds flying East, a Snake eating its tail, and a Jaguar — in the shop. Well, it seems pretty ordinary. What do you make of it, Mr. Artunian?
ARTUNIAN:	Nothing but profit. Let me look it up in Artunian's Automotive Guide to Fabled Lost Cities. Ah! Here it is. You, my fortunate friends, have stumbled onto the map to the Royal Inca Citadel of Axl Taxl! Lost for thousands of years! You see? Three birds flying East — that means enormous treasure! A snake eating its tail — danger to the unclean! And the sacred jaguar — camping facilities, chemical toilets and easy access to the Pan American Highway. Would you like me to book you on the next bus?

HARRY: Anyplace is better than Bat City! On to Axl Taxl. Say, what does that mean, anyway?

ARTUNIAN: Axl Taxl? Roughly translated — Bat City.

DR F: Come on, boys. I'll pay for the Toby Jug. Here, you Tasmanian devil!

ARTUNIAN: Keep your tongue, or I'll give you the back of my hand!

DR F: We'll take it!

ARTUNIAN: You want my hand? What for?

DR F: Because of that curious lavender spot just beneath your knuckle.

ARTUNIAN: Why, that's nothing but a birthmark my mother gave to me.

ARCHER: But, Dr. Firesign — we can't afford...

DR F: Quiet, old man! I've traveled this wide world over, ten thousand miles or more, but an authentic map of the fabled Lost City of Shangra Deelite on the back of an Armenian Shopkeeper's hand, I never done seen before.

ALL: Shangra Deelite!

DR F: Mr. Artunian, we want to buy your hand.

ARTUNIAN: My hand? My one remaining hand? This dear hand? Why all the perfumes in Arabia could not buy it! If you tickle it, does it not bleed? This wrist, this thumb, this index circled with a golden band, this fist, this sweaty palm, this hand. How much?

ARCHER: Well, we've only got a few dollars...

ARTUNIAN: Sold! Here, take it. But I'm afraid you'll have to wrap it yourself.

DR F: Gentlemen, thanks to Mr. Artunian's hand, we've been saved from Bat City, and we're off into the jungle in search of Shangra Deelite.

TRANSITION OF JUNGLE SOUNDS, ENDING WITH A ROAR

LEO: What's that?

ARCHER: It's a great horned carnivorous ibex.

HARRY: Good heavens!

SOUND OF A BIRD — SWISH AND CRY

LEO: What was that?

ARCHER: It's a Giant Sumatran Gliding Rat. Poisonous!

HARRY: It should be.

HORRIFIC NOISE

LEO: What was that?

DR F: That was Mr. Archer. He just fell into the rhino pit.

HARRY: I've had enough of this Zoo.

DR F: We're ready to face the jungle. Come on men.

SOUND OF BEATING DRUMS

ARCHER: I remember my last clash with a rhino. It was in the Portland Zoo in ought '19. It was a much smaller beast, of course, with only one horn...

DR F: Quiet, Mr. Archer! Don't you hear the drums? We must be in headhunter country. Who's got the map?

HARRY: I have. It's in my pocket, trying to steal my loose change.

DR F: Give it to me — Look! It's pointing back the way we came.

ARCHER: I think it's trying to tell us something.

HARRY: It's quivering. Its palm is all sweaty. This hand is really nervous. It's trying to make me bite its nails!

ARCHER: It's pointing to that tree on our right.

HARRY: But that tree was just on our left.

SOUND: DRUMS STOP

ARCHER: Listen. The drums have stopped.

DR F: That's no tree, boys! It's an Indigenous Headhunter.

LEO: How do you know?

DR F: I can tell by the brass plate on the trunk — "Homo Indigenous, Donated by Mrs. Gerald Fitzpatrick, In Memory of an Endless Summer at Newport, 1924."

ART: mrmrmrmrmrmrmr

DR F: Don't worry, Art. We'll guard you with your life! Everyone inside the buffalo! Here they come!

HARRY: I think they've spotted us!

DR F: Right! We're all covered with spots.

HEADHUNTER: Man, you really on the spot!

HARRY: We actors. You headhunters.

HEADHUNTER: Hmm. Ever since Inca go underground, we lonely, we look for heads. You give us a hand, man?

DR F: Yes, here's a man's hand.

HEADHUNTER: Aggggg! What bummer! (FADES OFF)

DR F: Thank god, they've gone!

ART: mrmrmrmrmrmrm

HARRY: Oh, they've upset poor Art!

ARCHER: Well, we could entertain him with Act Two of The Count of Monte Cristo. I've been rehearsing it for the last seven pages.

ART: mrmrmrmrmrmrmr

DR F: No, let's play him some music. What would you like to hear, Art?

ART: mrmrmrmrmrmrmr

LEO: What's his favorite group? The Buffalo Butter Conspiracy?

ART: mrmrmrmrmrmr

HARRY: No. What about the Jimmy Buffalo Experience?

ART: mrmrmrmrmrmr

ARCHER: The Rhinoceros Springfield?

ART: mrmrmrmrmrmr

DR F: Captain Beefheart and his Magic Buffalo?

ART: mrmrmrmrmrmr

HARRY: He's drooling. Quick, play it!

MUSIC: CAPTAIN BEEFHEART "ABBA ZABBA"

DR F: Gimme three...

ARCHER: I pass...

HARRY: I'll stick with what I've got...

LEO: Hit me!

PAUSE — SOCK!

LEO: Why, you cheatin' varmint! I saw you deal that Jack from the bottom of the deck. I want another hand!

DR F: Here, take this one.

LEO: Aggggggggggh!

ARCHER: What's this severed hand doing in the Last Chant Saloon?

DR F: What are *we* doing in the Last Chant Saloon?

HARRY: Hey, this is next week's show!

DR F: Where did we leave the plot for this week's show?

ARCHER: On page 15.

DR F: Well, it's too late to turn back now. Forward! Into the jungle! Forward!

ALL: Forward!

DR F: Wait a moment! Where are we going?

ARCHER: If someone will unclench this map from around my throat, I'll tell you...aggghhh!

LEO: What does it say?

ARCHER: The directions carefully concealed in this lavender birthmark can bring us no further in our search for Shangra Deelite.

LEO: Wait! The hand is trying to write something in the sand.

HARRY: Is it a love letter?

DR F: No, it's a message.

ARCHER: What does it say?

LEO:	U C N G T M O P A...you can get mo pay...
DR F:	It's speed writing!
ARCHER:	Who gave this hand an upper?
HARRY:	Ha! We've got the upper hand!
DR F:	And we're hopelessly lost in this steaming jungle!
LEO:	Anybody got any clams?
HARRY:	What are we going to do, now that the hand has no more to say?
ARCHER:	Let's follow that freeway over there.
DR F:	Too obvious.
ART:	mrmrmrmrmrmr! (MOVING OFF)
HARRY:	The buffalo's running away!
DR F:	Of course! Why didn't we think of it before? We'll follow that magnificent beast as he follows his own native instincts, reverting to the call of the wild, unhindered by the limitations of the over-conceptualized, convoluted, mechanistic modern mind of man!
APPLAUSE	
DR F:	After him!
LEO:	Dr. Firesign?
DR F:	What is it, Leo?
LEO:	He's gone.
GROANS	
OLD MAN:	Help! Help! Over here! Help! Help!

DR F: Quick, gentlemen! Follow that hysterical cry for help help!

ARCHER: Press on through the underbrush!

DR F: I've never liked the underbrush press!

SOUNDS OF CRASHING THROUGH UNDERBRUSH

LEO: Oh! Look at that horrible hairy man!

ARCHER: Why, the poor man must be completely out of his mind from the heat, wearing a heavy coat in this weather!

OLD MAN: Help me! I've got a buffalo on my back! Won't someone help me, please! If I get out of this, I promise I'll never smoke another drop! Give me a hand!

PAUSE...APPLAUSE

OLD MAN: No! No! Give me a hand!

DR F: Here, take this one!

OLD MAN: Why, where did you get this? It's just like my map, only the thumb's on the other side. At last! I have it all! For 40 years, I've been wandering through this steaming jungle with no clams and Artunian's right hand, in search of the Lost City of Shangra Deelite. And now — I'll just put both hands together... Ah! I see it all now! You just make a left turn instead of a right when you get to ARRRGGH!

ARCHER: The poor devil. Strangled by his own map. It nearly happened to me...

HARRY: What did the old man say? Ah, I remember! Turn left instead of right at ARRRGGH!

DR F: And here we are!

GASPS OF WONDER

LAMA:	(CHANTS) Don't die tonight. Call Shangra Deelite!
ARCHER:	Where did that voice come from?
LAMA:	Welcome gentle friends. Welcome to Shangra Deelite.
ALL:	Shangra Deelite!!
LAMA:	We deliver. Bring your shaggy four-legged friend, too. There's room for all in Shangra Deelite.
HARRY:	This is marvelous! Never have I seen a more beautiful place!
ARCHER:	It's like playing the last act of Camille, all rolled into one!
LAMA:	Playing? What's that?
DR F:	My dear man — we're actors.
LAMA:	Actors? What's that?
LEO:	You know — the bright lights. The grease paint, the glamour, the applause...
HARRY:	The curtain going up on the first act...
ARCHER:	You going up in the second act...
DR F:	The audience getting up in the third act...
HARRY:	The playwright giving up in the fourth act...
ARCHER:	The cast throwing up in the fifth act...
DR F:	And the sixth act...
ARCHER:	Bat City!
LAMA:	No offence, but I don't understand a word you're saying, and neither do any of my people assembled here before you.

HARRY: Look! In the amphitheater - finally, an audience worthy of us.

ARCHER: It's larger than the Winter Palace in Spring.

DR F: Gentlemen, do you think we could...

LAMA: Of course you can.

ARCHER: No, we can't. Where are we going to get The King? We always hire a local actor for that one line, but these people are too small to fit the costume.

DR F: But the show must go on.

LAMA: Show?

ART: mrmrmrmrmrmrmr

HARRY: Of course! We can use Art! He's a trooper.

DR F: But can he learn the line?

ARCHER: He's been practicing it for months! I've been holding book for him. He's ready.

DR F: Good! Get him into the King Louis the 13th costume. We're about to play for our greatest audience.

LAMA: Audience?

DR F: Go tell all of your people assembled here before us that they've just got to be some of the most beautiful people in the whole wide world!

LAMA: It's true. It's true. It's true.

ARCHER: And we love you. And you'll love us, if you'll just turn around and watch the show.

GENERAL HUBUB

DR F: Good evening. May I present for your edification and enjoyment, an evening with Dr. Firesign's Original Traveling Antique Theatre of the Plains and Buffalo Show, in their immortal classic, "Waiting For The Count of Monte Cristo, Or Someone Like Him." The Scene — another part of the street, outside the alley, under the cul-de-sac, adjoining the antechamber, near the courtyard, in the palace, by the moonlight, wa da doo dah. Guelph speaks...

HARRY: (WAKING) What place is this?

ARCHER: Never mind. You are in safe hands.

HARRY: Get your hands off me, old man. Do you know who I am?

ARCHER: Far better than you, Edmond Dantes. Know now the secret of your birth — you are the only legitimate son of...

DAGGER TOSSED INTO BACK

ARCHER: ...of...agggggagagagagghhh! (DIES)

HARRY: I don't know any aaaaghgghggghh! My father's name was urrrrrgh. (AFTER A SILENCE) Dr. Firesign — they hate us out there!

DR F: Quick! Cut to the dueling scene.

LEO: Ah ha! Dantes! Here you are! And here I am! Take that, you swine!

HARRY: Why, this is not my swine!

LEO: Then take that, you blackguard!

CLANG! CLANG! CLANG! CLANG! CLANG!

STRUGGLE — HEAVY BREATHING

CLANG! CLANG!

SWORD SWISHES IN EMPTY AIR — PROLONGED DEATH CRIES — THUD

HARRY: They hate us, Dr. Firesign! We're dying! Cut to the poison scene, they always love that... Bon jour M. Hemloque. (Now to fix this traitorous dog of mine Uncle with some of his own medicine!) Sur la table!

DR F: Nephew!

HARRY: Gesundheit!

DR F: Is it not time that we spoke of your late father's will?

HARRY: Isn't it a little late for that? But first — let us share a churning flagon of burgundy.

DOOK DOOK DOOK

DR F: (He thinks he has me!)

FIZZZZZZZZ

HARRY: You first.

FIZZZZZZZZ

DR F: Just like his brother-in-law. Heavy on the hemlock. Well — here's to you, sister. (DRINKS) And now, while he is buckling his buckskin, I shall just take my dagger from my (WHOOPS AND CRIES AS HE GOES MAD, DIES)

HARRY: We're dying! They hate us! Oh, look — bring on the King! Bring on the king! It's the only thing that'll save us at this point.

SOUND: FANFARE

ARCHER: His Majesty, the King!

ART: mrmrmrmrmrmrmr

HARRY: Father!

ART:	mrmrmrmrmrmrmr

BURST OF APPLAUSE AND BRAVOS

VOICES:	Magnificent! The buffalo! We want the buffalo! Bring back the buffalo!
LAMA:	Now we know what acting is. You're terrible! But the buffalo is Brilliant! We've decided to let you off with your lives, if you'll leave the buffalo here.
DR F:	At last! We've found a place where Art is appreciated. Well, gentlemen, we might as well push on. There's nothing left for us but Bat City.
LAMA:	What did you say?
DR F:	Bat City.
LAMA:	But you've just played Bat City. Shangra Deelite means, in our language, "gathering place of the sub-audible flying mouse."
DR F:	Well, Mr. Archer?
ARCHER:	Yes, Dr. Firesign?
DR F:	After all these years, we've finally played Bat City.
ARCHER:	From now on it's all uphill.
BOY:	Hey! Dr. Firestein! I got another telegram for you or your buffalo.
DR F:	I'll take it, boy.
BOY:	You sure will! Stand back, it's another singing one. It's from all the people of Shangra Deelite. 1 — 2 — 3 -
VOICES:	(SINGING, TO MICKEY MOUSE CLUB THEME): B A T — C I T — Y — Spells bye to you. So long! Good bye!

ANNOUNCER: Firesign Theatre has just presented NONE OF THE ABOVE. Do you believe in buffalos? Say quick that you believe. If you believe, clap your hands!

ART: mrmrmrmrmrmrmr...

THEME MUSIC IN, UP AND OUT

Merry Xmas
PS

TILE IT LIKE IT IS
The Firesign Christmas Pageant

Performed live at the Magic Mushroom and broadcast on KRLA-AM on December 24, 1967.

ORIGINAL CAST

Philip Austin as Scipio, Conspirator 2, Soothsayer, Gluteus, Publius, Colitus, Conspirator 4, McNally, Ceramicus, Tribune, Rochester, Moroccan, Citizen, Melchior

Peter Bergman as Silius, Caesar, Cinna, Conspirator 3, Cannabis, Pythagorhombus, Martha, Balthazar

David Ossman as Announcer, Conspirator 1, Senator, Lucilius, Sibelius, Conspirator 5, Ptolemy, Caspar

Phil Proctor as Pretorius, Trebonius, Thrombosis, Caliyuga

TILE IT LIKE IT IS
The Firesign Christmas Pageant

RECORD:	ALEX NORTH — SPARTACUS "MAIN TITLE"
ANNOUNCER:	The Firesign Theatre presents TILE IT LIKE IT IS, an historical drama drawn from the later writings of Gibbon...
SOUND:	GO APE
MUSIC UP AND UNDER	
ANN:	The time - 83 A.D.
VOICE:	B.C.
ANN:	A.B.C.
VOICE:	A.B.C. what?
VOICE 2:	A.B.C.D. goldfish.
VOICE 3:	L.M.N.O. goldfish!
VOICE:	O.S.P.Q.R.
ANN:	Rome! The spleen of the mighty Empire, where from the towering heights of Capitoline Hill, the decisions that control the destiny of the Westerned World are nammened, and decrees of Imperial Margarine are handed down daily from the stately Senate's halls of marble...
SILIUS:	Hey, Scipio, I just won your aggie!

SCIPIO: My big orange aggie? I'll trade you all my steelies for it, Silius — and this cat's eye.

SILIUS: This is a very nice cat's eye (MEOW) — and the cat's attached. Where are the steelies?

SCIPIO: Inside the cat.

SILIUS: What can I do with a 50-pound cat?

SCIPIO: Throw it at the Emperor. Here he comes.

SOUND: TRUMPETS

ALL: Caesar! Caesar! Hail Caesar!

VOICE: Caesar!

SOUND: WOMAN SCREAMS

VOICE: Let go of her, swine!

VOICE 2: That's not her swine, it's my wife's! What'll you trade me for her?

VOICE: Here, catch!

SOUND: CAT MEOWS AND THUMPS

VOICE 2: This cat weighs a ton! And its hair is all matted!

VOICE: Send it to the catacombs!

SOUND: TRUMPET CALLS

ALL: Hail, Caesar! May you reign forever!

CONSPIRATOR 1: Hail and rain! It's a bad omen, for a Roman.

CONSPIRATOR 2: Even his best friends won't kill him.

CONSPIRATOR 1: Shhhhh! Caesar speaks!

CAESAR: My fellow Romans...

SOOTHSAYER: Beware the Hares of March!

CAESAR: Who's that? Guards, bring that blind, ragged soothsayer here before the mighty Caesar!

VOICES: MUMBLE MUMBLE

CAESAR: Speak, ancient prophet!

SOOTHSAYER: Beware the Hares of March!

CAESAR: You must be mad!

SOOTHSAYER: If you do not believe me, read what is written in the entrails of this March Hare!

CAESAR: You, Pretorius...

VOICE: No, me Tarzan!

CAESAR: Oh, sorry — you, Pretorius, spilt this hare.

PRETORIUS: Hail Caesar!

SOUND: SCHWICK

SOOTHSAYER: Entrails, entrails! Read all about it!

CAESAR: I can divine from the condition of the liver that this rabbit is drunk!

VOICE: No, the entrails! Read the entrails, Caesar!

CAESAR: Oh. All right. "Flavia, come home and get a grip on yourself!" Signed, your loving husband, Agrippa. Wait a minute! This is the classified entrails!

VOICE: You've got the Sunday rabbit, Caesar!

CAESAR: Oh — give me the funnies.

SOUND: UGLY SHPLOP

CAESAR: Eggh!

VOICE: Read me Little Orphan Entrails!

VOICE 2: Save me Terry and the Pancreas!

VOICE 3: I wanna hear the Katzenjammer Kidneys!

CAESAR: I read no evil portents in this hare, soothsayer.

SOOTHSAYER: Then beware of Harry Katz!

CAESAR: Why?

SOOTHSAYER: Because I'm going to kill you. I'm Harry Katz!

CAESAR DIES

ROMAN: Oh, horror! The Emperor is dead!

GENERAL HUBUB

SENATOR: Senators! The news of the Emperor's death saddens us all.

APPLAUSE

SENATOR: But we cannot let our grief intervene in necessary prosecution of our civic responsibilities. Therefore, we must perform the tedious but necessary ritual so vital to the stabilization and perpetuation of the Roman Empire. We must, in sober council and with all deliberate speed, elect a new Emperor.

VOICE: All right! Everybody put your heads down on your desks! No peeking! All in favor of Gluteus Maximus, raise your hands. (COUNTING) Sixty-one. Now, everybody in favor of Various Flavius, say Aye. (counts) I, II, III...

VOICE 2: (SINGS, TO "CIELITO LINDO") Aye, aye, aye! I vote for Flavius!

VOICE: ...IV...

VOICE 3: He's got the Ivy League vote.

VOICE: ...V, VI... XXXI. Various Flavius has 31.

SENATOR: Gluteus Maximus is the new Emperor. And Various Flavius is the new Hall Monitor.

ALL: All hail Caesar Gluteus!

GLUTEUS: My fellow Romans! It is a great honor for me as your new Emperor to inaugurate my reign with the performance of my first act. Maestro, please... (SINGS) Way down upon the Tiber River, that's where I long to Ro-man...

APPLAUSE

GLUTEUS: Second act — (SINGS) Hold That Tiber!... But my third act! It will amuse and delight you to hear that I hereby order the immediate strangulation of all those hated Proconsuls who have oppressed you these many years. Death to the proconsul of Galicia!

SOUND: AGGH

GLUTEUS: Death to the Proconsul of Lydia!

SOUND: AGGH

GLUTEUS: Death to the Proconsul of Cappadocia!

VOICE: Cappadocia? Caesar —

GLUTEUS: Yes!

VOICE: Are you sure?

GLUTEUS: As sure as I am Gluteus Maximus, Emperor of Rome, Regent of the Nile and Proconsul of Cappad... hey, wait a minute... (DIES)

ALL: Oh, horrors! The Emperor is dead!

SENATOR: Senators! Once again the news of the Emperor's death saddens us all.

APPLAUSE

SENATOR: But we cannot let our grief intervene...

VOICE: OK, OK, let's elect a new Emperor and get him over with!

SENATOR: Very well. Let us now, in true democratic process, nominate one of our august body —

VOICE: I nominate August Body!

SENATOR: Not yet! — to rule forever over this vast empire we call home. Do I hear any nominations?

PUBLIUS: I, Publius, nominate Trebonius.

TREBONIUS: I, Trebonius, nominate Publius.

LUCILIUS: I, Lucilius, nominate Cinna, the poet.

CINNA: I, Cinna, vote for the winna.

COLITUS: I, Colitus, nominate Thrombosis.

THROMBOSIS: (COUGH COUGH) I, Thrombosis...

SIBELIUS: I, Sibelius, nominate Delius.

VOICE: Delius' gone.

MOB (OUTSIDE): We want Caesar! We want Caesar!

SENATOR: No! No, Senators! This will never do! The crowd clamors for a new Caesar. Listen!

MOB (OUTSIDE): Caesar, we want a new Caesar! ROAR!

SENATOR: We must elect an Emperor before that mob breaks into the senate chambers. Who amongst us will dare to face that unruly rabble, quiet them, and bring order to the troubled streets of Rome?

CALIYUGA: Order? Unruly? I can handle them! Let me speak to them. I'd love to do it.

SENATOR: Who speaks? Ah, Caliyuga! The Junior Senator from Armenius. Go to it!

CALIYUGA: All right, friends, Romans, countrymen! I want all the Friends up in front, all the Romans in back, and all the countrymen line up over there and go back to the country.

MOB: ROARS

CALIYUGA: Oh yeah! Still milling and seething, huh? Okay, I want to see all the millers on the left, and the seethers on the right...

VOICE: Hail seethers, forsooth!

CALIYUGA: Who said that? All right, you! All you sooth-seethers gang up over there behind Harry Katz!

MOB OUT

SENATOR: Is Caliyuga gone? Can he hear us? Oh, have we got a surprise for him! Quick now, let's all take a vote. All those in favor of Caliyuga for Emperor, whisper Aye.

VOICES: Aye.

SENATOR: It's unanimous! Let's call him back in and tell him what he's won. Guards, go and bring him in.

VOICES: MUMBLE MUMBLE

CALIYUGA: That's the most unruly mob I've ever seen in my life! I was trying to get the big guys down in front and nobody would lend me their ears. Then threw them at me. If I only had the authority... Oh, excuse me fellow Senators! Did I interrupt your voting? You've all got your right hands raised and...

ALL: Hail Caesar!

CALIYUGA: Oh, yeah. Hail Caesar! Who's the pigeon?

ALL: Hail, Emperor Caliyuga!

CALIYUGA: Oh-oh! You mean... Oh, you sneaky guys! Is that the best plan you could come up with? Electing me while I was out of the chamber? Boy, can't you do anything according to the rules? If you'd asked me, like a true Roman, I might have accepted, but so long as I'm Emperor, there's going to be some changes made around here! First of all...

CONSPIRATOR 3: I think the time has come.

CONSPIRATOR 4: Hand me my bludgeon.

CONSPIRATOR 5: Here's the cat.

SOUND: CAT MEOWS

CONSPIRITOR 3: Give me my knife. Ooop! No, you dummy! How many times have I told you — handle first!

CALIYUGA: About this assassination, for instance.

CONSPIRATOR 4: I think he's on to us.

CONSPIRATOR 5: Hide the cat.

CONSPIRATOR 3: Put it in the catapult.

SOUND: CAT MEOWS THROUGH SPACE AND LANDS

CALIYUGA: Who threw that cat? What a rotten shot! If you can't do anything right, let's not do it at all. You want to have an assassination? Fine! All the bludgeoners over there by the statue of Jupiter. Poisoners, by the fresco depicting the assassination of Gluteus Maximus. Stranglers, lurk over there by the columns. Makes a nice balanced picture... And all the drowners into the pool! And now, you knife freaks, daggers up front, long knives in the middle and broadswords to the rear. Everybody in place? Now, I'll stand here. I'll lift my arm — I could sprawl like this... (AD LIBS)

VOICES: What a bummer... Let's go... He's no fun... We can't assassinate him...

ALL: Long live the Emperor! And we really mean it... (MUMBLING OFF)

CALIYUGA: Well, I'm glad they're gone — but they certainly left a mess. Just look at that pile of junk over there in the corner. You two there! Who are you?

PTOLEMY: We're your closest advisors.

CALIYUGA: Yes, it is a little close in here. Follow me into the Imperial bath, and we'll discuss the present and future state of the Empire.

SOUND: SPLASHING

CALIYUGA: Ah, nothing feels better after a hard day of putting things in order than to relax in a scented bath and wash the blood off one's hands. What's in this delicious bath?

PTOLEMY: Warm mulled goat's milk scented with ambergris.

CALIYUGA: Ah, you must be my faithful advisor Tolemy.

PTOLEMY: P-tolemy.

CALIYUGA: Gesundheit.

PTOLEMY: P-thank you.

CALIYUGA: Ptolemy, what is ambergris?

PTOLEMY: Whale p-vomit.

CALIYUGA: Oh. Fine. Let's just swim over to the next bath. Ah! The steam bath. What is it scented with?

CANABIS: Grape leaves, oh mighty Caesar. Here, roll your own.

CALIYUGA: Hold on there — I'd recognize this leaf anywhere. It's from my laurel wreath.

CANABIS: That's right, Caesar. The grapes of wreath.

CALIYUGA: Stein back! I can't see you through that haze of smoke... Why, you're head of my Praetorian guard, Canabis Lapid!

CANABIS: Here to protect and to serve! LAPD. SPQR.

CALIYUGA: Well, now that you're all here — let's get down to business. Soap my back and tell me how goes the empire.

CANABIS: From left to right.

CALIYUGA: Good! Ptolemy, bring me a map so that I may see the extent of our conquests to date.

PTOLEMY: You want to date the conquests, Caesar?

CALIYUGA: Bring the map, you puffoon!

PTOLEMY: My assistant is swimming over with it now.

MCNALLY: (OFF) (SINGING, TO "LOCH LOMOND") Oh, you take the high road, and I'll take the low road...

CALIYUGA: Look at this. This is soggy.

PTOLEMY: No, that's Gaul.

CALIYUGA: What I mean is, the Empire's in a soggy state! What are its boundaries?

PTOLEMY:	From the northern beaches of Conius Isle, your possessions do extend here through the Lands of Gitchigoomia, by the shining big sea waters, past the Straights of Nicodemus, to the Squares of Timbucktoo.
MCNALLY:	Three.
PTOLEMY:	Three.
CALIYUGA:	But all of these provinces are irregularly shaped. It's so sloppy. And there are so many of them.
MCNALLY:	The borders are fixed by nature's own design — mountains, trees, lakes...
CALIYUGA:	But look at the colors! The colors are all different. It's terrible. Gaul is vermilion, Hibernia is plaid, Germania is gray, Nubia is black, Lebanon is green...
CANABIS:	Sure is!
CALIYUGA:	And they're painting the passports brown! It's all one Empire — why isn't it all one color? Who's responsible for drawing this map?
PTOLEMY:	It was scribed on sheepskin by this teeny weeny barbarian from the North — Randy McNally.
MCNALLY:	Aye, that's me.
CALIYUGA:	Well, you're a cute little fellow. But I'm telling you now, there are going to be some changes made here! And fast! Change it! I want it all blue!
PTOLEMY:	Very well, Caesar. McNally — repaint that map.
CALIYUGA:	No, Ptolemy — not the map. I'm speaking of the Empire itself. (SINGS, TO "THERE'LL BE SOME CHANGES MADE") There'll be a change in Dalmatia and a change in Gaul — from now on, I'm going to change it all. (SPLASH — BLUB)
CANABIS:	Hail Caesar! The Praetorian Guards are at your service.

I shall assemble the legions from far and wide. We'll begin by painting the Mediterranean aquamarine...

MCNALLY: (SINGS) Oh, you paint the highroad and I'll paint the low road! (AD LIBS)

CALIYUGA: No, no! Doesn't anybody understand me? Listen — you can't cover the boundless oceans, the stately mountains, the endless stretches of limitless desert, the green and fertile virgin forests, the fruited plains, the ripe olive tree groves with paint! Do you think that even I would dare to defy nature's gods? Do you think me a madman? Ha ha ha ha! Paint the Empire? Absurd! Tile it!

PTOLEMY: You mean — tile it? With tiles?

CALIYUGA: Yes, isn't it beautiful? Just like this bath.

CANABIS: But this bath is covered with one-inch-square mosaic tiles.

CALIYUGA: Yes, isn't it pretty? Canabis! I now decree the Mosaic Law! (SINGS, TO "SMILES") "There are tiles that make me happy, there are tiles that make me blue!" And I want them all blue!

MCNALLY: The Mosaic blue laws!

CALIYUGA: No, not blue blue! Baby blue! (BLUB BLUB) Now, get out! All of you! Leave my presence!

MCNALLY: We'll put them under the tree...

CALIYUGA: Ah! At last! Nothing can stand in the way of my childhood dream coming true. A symmetrically perfect, completely ordered world done entirely in baby blue. I can see for tiles, and tiles and tiles... (BLUB BLUB)

RECORD: JIM KWESKIN AND THE JUG BAND "BLUES MY NAUGHTY SWEETIE GIVES TO ME"

PTOLEMY: And so you see, Ceramicus, Emperor Caliyuga has decreed — er — that the whole Empire be tiled. Entiley. How long do you think it will take?

CERAMICUS: Well, Rome was built in a day. This should take about a week. How many tiles will we need for the job?

PTOLEMY: Well, Pythagorhombus, as the esteemed, official, Empirical Mathematician, you should have the answer.

PYTHAG: Yes, I should. Let me calculate. In a Right Empire, the sum of all the squares on both sides of the...let's see... Triangle 7-5583... In Nubia Jersey call collectus... Ptolemy, what's MCLXXVI minus CVMXXIV?

PTOLEMY: CLXMIIV. Give or take an IIV.

PYTHAG: Precisely. You'll need eight billion to the third power tiles. Give or take a crock of tile.

CERAMICUS: Here, take one.

PTOLEMY: Ow! That's not a crockatile, that's a hippopotenuse!

PYTHAG: No, that's a square of a hippopotenuse. Look, it's wearing brown shoes!

PTOLEMY: Then it's decided. The Emperor demands that all the tiles be blue.

CERAMICUS: That's no problem. We have the greatest selection of blue tiles in the Empire. Look at this one from Pompeii!

ALL: Ooooo, wow!

CERAMICUS: And here's one from Ghent.

PYTHAG: Oh, a Ghent tile!

SOUND: DING DING

TRIBUNE: The Emperor comes from the Coliseum. All prepare to hail!

PYTHAG: Why, it's the Tribune. Hi, Herald!

PTOLEMY: Oh, it's the Herald Tribune. I thought you were dead.

TRIBUNE: I bring you news of the World, the Telegram and the Sun!

PYTHAG: I'll subscribe to the world and the sun, but I decline the telegram.

TRIBUNE: You can't decline the telegram.

PYTHAG: Of course I can. Telegram, telegras, telegrat, telegramma, tellegrampa, telantrhody... (THEY RAZZ HIM) That's nothing. Would you like to hear the decline of Rome?

SOUND: TRUMPETS

PTOLEMY: Here he comes now.

ALL: Hail Caesar! Hail Caliyuga!

CALIYUGA: Ah, good! You're all here, my noble counselors. I've just been to the Coliseum. You ought to see the games people play!

PTOLEMY: Did you have good seats?

CALIYUGA: Yes, right in the Caesarian section. It was a magnificent inauguration, capped by an Assyrian acrobat — or a Syrian acrobat — the program wasn't clear, it was written in Igpay Atinlay. At any rate, he leapt from the top of a flaming tower, a thousand cubits from the ground, without a parachute.

PTOLEMY: What's a parachute?

CALIYUGA: I don't know. He didn't have one.

CERAMICUS: Hail Caesar!

CALIYUGA: Thank you!

CERAMICUS: I, Ceramicus —

CALIYUGA: I'm sorry to hear that.

CERAMICUS: ...shall display before you all the varieties of blue tile to be had in the Empire.

CALIYUGA: Good! I have a particular color in mind, however. Let's see...no, no, no, no — none of these! Have you nothing else?

CERAMICUS: No, great Caesar. That's every conceivable shade of blue in the world...

PTOLEMY: Except of course for the fabled Moroccan blue.

CANABIS: Yeah, Moroccan blue!

CALIYUGA: Wait! Morocco, Morocco — yes! The blue men of Morocco! Ptolemy — was I not born in Morocco?

PTOLEMY: No.

CALIYUGA: Well, so what! Let's go there anyway. Canabis!

CANABIS: Gezundheit!

CALIYUGA: Thank you! Assemble the Legions, we're on the road to Morocco. Get Bing, Bob, Dorothy and Toto and let's be off!

RECORD: ALEX NORTH — SPARTACUS "MAIN TITLE"

SOUND: TRUMPETS AND HORSES

CALIYUGA: Say, Canabis...

CANABIS: Canabis.

CALIYUGA: Thank you.

CANABIS: You're welcome.

CALIYUGA: Look, there before us — is those the fabled enameled gate of Morocco? Are those the fabled enameled gate of

Morocco? Fabled gate of Morocco, enameled those is? Damn, I wish I could learn to speak Latin. Well, is it?

CANABIS: Is it what?

CALIYUGA: What I said.

CANABIS: No.

CALIYUGA: No what?

CANABIS: No, it's not Morocco.

CALIYUGA: But we should be there by now.

CANABIS: Be where?

CALIYUGA: Beware of what?

CANABIS: Here!

CALIYUGA: Where we are?

CANABIS: Where's that?

CALIYUGA: That's what I'm asking you! Damn, I wish I could speak Latin!

ROCHESTER: Mr. Benny? That's the Arch of Tiberius.

CANABIS: We must be outside of Rochester.

CALIYUGA: Well!

PTOLEMY: Wait a minute! We've been traveling for twenty days, and we're only just outside of Rochester?

CALIYUGA: Well, all roads lead to Rochester.

ROCHESTER: Great Caesar's ghost, Mr. Benny!

PTOLEMY: Stop that!

CANABIS: Did that slave say Benny? Who's got the bennies?

CALIYUGA: Legions of Rome! Forward to Morocco with all deliberate speed!

CANABIS: Speed? Did that man say speed?

ROCHESTER: I'll deliber it in just a minute.

CALIYUGA: Now cut that out! Oh Don! Don, you and Dennis form a phalanx...oh, sorry. Legionnaires! Form your phalanx and follow the directions in this book!

CANABIS: Why?

CALIYUGA: Because it's Morocco bound!

RECORD: ALEX NORTH — SPARTACUS "MAIN TITLE"

SOUND: TRUMPETS DRUMS AND HORSES

CALIYUGA: Well, Canabis, we've traveled over 8000 leagues. Aren't we in Morocco yet?

CANABIS: Well, Caesar, they're only little leagues. Wait a minute...let me check... (SNIFFS) Yes, Caesar, I think we've arrived! Why look, here come the Vandals to greet us!

PTOLEMY: Who's that woman leading them?

CANABIS: That's Martha.

CALIYUGA: Martha and the Vandals — listen! They're singing for us!

MARTHA AND THE VANDALS (SINGING):

Attila was sitting on his hairy throne.
(He's a Hun. He's number one.)
He said come on boys, let's make it down to Rome!
(Let's go to town, let's burn it down.)
And then we'll go down to Rome and then we'll come
right back,

(We're coming back, we're on the track.)
He said come on horde — (SNAP SNAP) — let's sack!

CALIYUGA: Hun-hun-hun-do-do-do-do-hun

CALIYUGA + MARTHA:
Do the Hun — it's what the latest rage is.
Do the Hun — it's from the Golden ages.
No other dance can touch it,
No other holds a candle,
I learned it from a Visigoth,
Who learned it from a Vandal.
Do the Hun...

CALIYUGA: Wait a minute! Wait a minute! Will someone please tell me — where are the blue men?

MARTHA: They're all at the gathering of the Tribes.

CALIYUGA: Gathering of the tribes?

MARTHA: Yeah, man — the Barbari-In.

PTOLEMY: I don't see anything but a lot of people riding camels.

MARTHA: No, man — that's the Bedou-In. Over there.

CANNABIS: You mean the dancing bear?

MARTHA: No, man — that's the Hanna Barari-In. Over there, where the smoke is coming from.

PTOLEMY: Ah! Smokey the Bearbarian!

CALIYUGA: All right! Soldiers of Rome, dismount and disport yourselves.

ALL: What?

CALIYUGA: Canabis, and Ptolemy, come with me to the tent of the blue men. At last I will find the shade of blue that we've traveled such a vast distance for, crossing impassible mountains and impossible puns. There!

There, Ptolemy, is their tent. You see, it's been blew over. Oh, I wish I could speak Latin! Now I've blown it. It's blue all over. Let's open the tent flap...

MOROCCAN: (SINGS, TO "BLUE MOON") Blue man — you saw me standing alone...

CALIYUGA: No! That's not it at all! They're not the right color blue! We've traveled all this way for nothing. Oh, Ptolemy, my noble counselor, help me.

PTOLEMY: Well, Caesar, lie down here on this sand dune and try and remember your childhood...

CALIYUGA: All right. Let me see... I see — I see a shield!

PTOLEMY: A blue shield?

CALIYUGA: No.

PTOLEMY: A shield with a blue cross?

CALIYUGA: No, it's a silver shield with blue-crossed eyes!

PTOLEMY: They're your eyes, reflected in your father's shield!

APPLAUSE

CALIYUGA: Or — they're my father's eyes reflected in my shield!

APPLAUSE

PTOLEMY: But, Caesar — you didn't have a father.

CANABIS: And he didn't have a shield.

CALIYUGA: Then they're my eyes! I see! I see! The color I'm looking for is not just the blue of a baby's eyes but the blue of a royal baby's eyes! Royal Baby Blue! I must find a royal, blue-eyed baby!

CITIZEN: Excuse me, great Caesar, but I couldn't help overhearing you. You're lying on me.

CALIYUGA: Caesar never lies. Hold your tongue, citizen.

CITIZEN: (WITH TONGUE BETWEEN FINGERS) Well, if you're looking for an astrologer, there's one over there in that tent.

CALIYUGA: Psst, Ptolemy — what did he psay?

PTOLEMY: He said, there's an astrologer in that tent over there who can help us.

CALIYUGA: Let us consult him immediately. Knock on the tent.

CANABIS: How do you knock on a tent?

CALIYUGA: Announce me, then.

CANABIS: Great Caesar stands without!

CASPAR: Well, give him a little something, please.

MELCHIOR: Come inside, mighty Caesar.

CALIYUGA: Why, what a lovely tent.

BALTHAZAR: Kindly be seated, Caliyuga.

CASPAR: May we be perhaps of some assistance to you...

CALIYUGA: Yes, mighty astrologers. I'm looking for a royal, blue-eyed baby.

MELCHOIR: What a coincidence. So are we.

BALTHAZAR: For seven years, the three of us have been traveling from Persia, anticipating his birth.

CASPAR: And it's going to happen any day now.

MELCHOIR: Probably tomorrow.

CALIYUGA: How do you know about this royal child?

BALTHAZAR: We've been reading all about him — in the Morning Star.

CASPAR: I have drawn his chart. He has everything rising.

CALIYUGA: Can you tell me, holy man! His eyes — will his eyes be truly royal baby blue?

MELCHOIR: Yes. His eyes will be truly blue.

CALIYUGA: How can I find him? Where can I see him?

BALTHAZAR: Be patient, mighty Caesar. Soon, very soon, he will come to you.

CALIYUGA: But my dream — my great plan — I was going to tile...

CASPAR: Don't worry, Caesar. We know all about that.

MELCHOIR: Yes, yes — soon you will see everything realized.

CASPAR: Melchoir, it is midnight...

CALIYUGA: Midnight?

BALTHAZAR: Aaah — it's all over now — baby blue.

SINGERS: God rest ye, merry gentlemen, let nothing you dismay, Remember Christ our savior was born on Christmas Day.

CONTINUE HUMMING UNDER

ANN: The Firesign Theatre has presented TILE IT LIKE IT IS, a Christmas pageant. God bless us, every one.

SINGERS: O, tidings of comfort and joy, comfort and joy...

RECORD: BEATLES "YOUR MOTHER SHOULD KNOW"

THE FIRESIGN TH

A LIFE IN THE DAY

Performed live at the Magic Mushroom and broadcast on KRLA-AM on January 14, 1968. Written by The Firesign Theatre.

This is the first version of a day of television broadcasting that became "The TV Set," performed at the Ash Grove in 1969 and on tour on the East Coast in early 1970, and which formed the background for Firesign's 1970 LP "Don't Crush That Dwarf, Hand Me The Pliers."

ORIGINAL CAST

Phil Austin as Hugh Downer, George, the Judge, Dad, Neal, Pat Boone, Felix Paparazzi, Ida Matetsky, High Pockets, Les, M. C.

Peter Bergman as Patti Pap, Jim, Assistant D.A., Walter Klondike, Bob, Hunk, Vespasian, Sol, Father O'Long

David Ossman as Marvin, Kathy, Mrs. Napalmolive, Henry, Joyce, Gunderson's Announcer, Bronco, Hercules, Tony Gomez

Phil Proctor as Mike, Doc, Sailor Bill, Lawyer, Mary, Sgt. Spotless, Ozzie, General Klein, Madge, George Matetsky, Jehova, Jewish Comic, Vera Lamont, Ralph, Tenor

A LIFE IN THE DAY

ANNOUNCER: The Firesign Theatre presents A LIFE IN THE DAY.

SOUND: SNORING — ALARM RING — ALARM OFF — YAWNS

VOICE: Turn it off. (TOKES) Turn it on.

SOUND: CLICK — WHITE NOISE — TONE

ANNOUNCER: Good morning. Station KWKW-T-TV, Indian Grave, Montana, begins its broadcast day. KWKW-T-TV is owned and operated by the Firesign Theatre Broadcasting Company, with studios and transmitters located high atop the Piute Mound. Portions of today's programming are prerecor...

SOUND: MUSIC BOX AND TICK TOCK

HUGH: Good morning. I'm Hugh Downer...

PATTI: And I'm Patti Pap...

HUGH: And this is "Today's Day Today."

PATTI: This is Monday, January 29th. What happened today in history, Hugh?

HUGH: Well, Patti, on this day in 1776, the Peace of Lucerne was signed, ending the 40 Years War, and the plague broke out in Lisbon. In 1898, America's first musical show, "The Black Crook", opened at the old Henry Hudson Theatre on Little West Eighth Street.

PATTI: Famous people born today include Jack Larue, George Matetsky, the Beatles, and Marvin Fengleman — our producer.

THEY SING: HAPPY BIRTHDAY TO YOU

MARVIN (OFF): Thanks, kids!

HUGH: Marvin's been producing this show for 26 years, Patti, do you know that?

MARVIN (OFF): 27.

HUGH: Well, it's — what? 27 years. Patti, it's National Groundnut Day in South Carolina, open season on bobolinks starts in the Midwest, and I know we must have a lot of viewers in Iowa watching us from their trailers, guns oiled and ready.

PATTI: Get a few for me, boys.

HUGH: And, Patti — do you know what else today is?

PATTI: Yes, Hugh. It's Unification Day.

HUGH: It was just a year ago today when War President Johnson was given the Mandate.

PATTI: That's why the flags are at half mast and all the banks are open.

HUGH: How's the weather, Patti?

PATTI: Well, Hugh — that cold front from Alaska today has moved into the Gulf of California due to the disappearance last night of the Sierra Nevada Mountains, so the smog alert is lifted for all you folks on the East Coast. You can look forward to one to two inches of grey snow and three hours of deep breathing.

HUGH: Thanks, Patti. We'll be back in one minute with a fascinating demonstration by members of the Royal

Swedish Leather Belt and Whip Corps, opening tonight at the Winter Palace Theater.

PATTI: And I'll be having some girl-chat with their leader, Madam Olga, about her private impressions on American men.

HUGH: But first, this message...

SOUND: CUPS

KATHY: Mike? Another cup of coffee for you?

MIKE: No thanks, honey. I've had enough.

KATHY: How about you, George?

GEORGE: No thanks, darling. I've had enough, too.

KATHY: How about you, Jim?

JIM (SPADE): No thanks, baby. I'm full up.

SOUND: HARMONICA RUN

KATHY: (SOBS)

DOC: What seems to be the matter, Kathy?

KATHY: Well, Dr. Gunderson, I've been living with the guys for almost two months now, and everything's worked out wonderfully. Except...

DOC: Ya?

KATHY: They don't want it anymore, Dr. Gunderson.

DOC: Don't want what, child?

KATHY: My coffee — they're tired of my coffee!

DOC: It's ban pretty clear that your coffee lacks Zest Appeal.

KATHY:	Zest Appeal? What's that?
DOC:	Dat's the secret ingredient in Ersatz Brothers Coffee — ya! A blend of the finest Brazilian coffee beans, Chilean chicory nuts and Spanish flies. Here, take this can home with you, Kathy.
KATHY:	Well, all right, I'll try it.
SOUND:	HARMONICA RUN
KATHY:	Well, boys — would you like another cup of coffee?
BOYS:	(SIP COFFEE) OH LAY!
KATHY:	(SIGHS)
SOUND:	XYLOPHONE RUN
ANNOUNCER:	Ersatz Brothers Coffee — with Zest Appeal. Look for the can in the plain brown can.
BOYS:	O.K.! Ersatz!
SOUND:	XYLOPHONE STING
ANNOUNCER:	This is KWKW-T-TV, Channel One, River-rat Heights, Kansas. At the tone (BEEP) the time will be 11 AM.
RECORD CUE:	TEDDY BEARS PICNIC
ANNOUNCER:	Hey, kids! What time is it?
KIDS:	It's Gumdrop Time!
ANNOUNCER:	That's right! And here he comes now, down the licorice schtick gangplank of the Good Ship Gumdrop. It's Sailor Bill!
SOUND:	TOOT-TOOT
BILL:	Hi, Gumdroppers!

KIDS:	Hi, Sailor Bill!
BILL:	Let's all drop our gum. (LAUGHS) Just kidding. (OFF MIKE LAUGH) The crew — the camera crew — is a little happier than usual today. What have you been dropping, fellas? (TOOT-TOOT) I know why Charlie's laughing. It's his anniversary today. How many years has it been, Charlie? (OFF-MIKE MUMBLE) 17 years. That's wonderful. I hope your kids should live so long. And now, before we see our first cartoon, let's visit the wonderful world of Cartell Toys, with a lovely surprise for all you girls and boys...
RECORD CUE:	MARCH VERSION OF NATIONAL GUARD
ANNOUNCER:	By day — a secret underwater camera! (CLICK CLICK) In the afternoon, an infrared telescope and signaling mirror. (BEEP BEEP) By night, a deadly weapon! (BANG BANG) THE AVENGER!!
ANNOUNCER 2:	THE AVENGER! Cartell Toys' newest escalation in the ever-widening neighborhood arms race. Be the first on your block to get one — if you want to be the last!
ANNOUNCER:	THE AVENGER! Get it — before it gets you!
ANNOUNCER 2:	From Cartell Toys.
SOUND:	XYLOPHONE STING
RECORD CUE OUT	
BILL:	And THE AVENGER would make a wonderful birthday present too. So we're going to send one to these lucky gumdroppers who sent in their cards by the deadline. Jimmy Guercio, Georgie Matetsky and Sally Ann Ching. Be on the way in just a few hours. And by the way, kids — guess who else has a birthday today?... Me. I'm 38. That's right, Charlie. I'm 38 years old today. And I'm standing here in a sailor suit. Yeah...and let's get to the cartoon right now. What is

	it? Tweetie and Sylvester. Let's see what they're up to today. Roll it! (SLIDE WHISTLE) Happy birthday. 38!...
KAZOO:	FANFARE
WHISTLE:	PEER GYNT
KAZOO:	SUSPENSE THEME
BIRD VOICE:	Oh, oh!
SOUND:	CAR APPROACHING — SCREECH — CRASH
VOICES:	ANGRY CAT AND DOG CHASE
KAZOO:	CHASE THEME UNDER
SOUND:	EXPLOSIONS UNDER — DOOR SLAM
CAT VOICE:	PANTING — SIGH OF RELIEF
SOUND:	HISS OF FUSE
CAT VOICE:	Oh, oh!
SOUND:	MUFFLED EXPLOSION
CAT VOICE:	HOWL OF PAIN
KAZOO:	PEER GYNT
BIRD WHISTLES:	WHISTLE WHILE YOU WORK
SOUND UNDER:	HAMMERING AND SAWING
KAZOO:	SNEAKY MUSIC
CAT VOICE:	APPROACHING MEOWS — SUMMONING WHISTLES
BIRD VOICE:	Oh, oh!

SOUND:	RAPID SAWING
CAT VOICE:	Oh, oh!
SOUND:	CAT FALLS (BOB WHISTLE) — SPLASH OF WATER
BIRD WHISTLES:	WILD BLUE YONDER
SOUND:	AIRPLANE MOTOR STARTING — TAKES OFF
BIRD WHISTLES:	HIGH AND THE MIGHTY
KAZOO:	AIRPLANE ATTACKS
BIRD VOICE:	Oh, oh!
SOUND:	AIRPLANES — GUNFIRE — FLAK — BOMBS
SOUND:	AIRPLANE SHOT DOWN — CAT FLOATING DOWN AND LANDING
KAZOO:	SNEAKY MUSIC
BIRD WHISTLE:	SUMMONING WHISTLE
CAT VOICE:	Oh, oh!
SOUND:	GUN WITH SILENCER
CAT VOICE:	DYING
KAZOO:	SIGNATURE MUSIC
VOICE OVER:	That's All Folks!
KAZOO:	FANFARE ENDING
BILL:	Wasn't that fun, kids? Well, gumdroppers, we're going to be seeing more of our favorite cartoon characters right after another wonderful playtime surprise from the Little Old Toymaker — Cartell Industries, Inc. In business for over 35 years — just like me...

VOICES (SINGING):	FRERE JACQUES (UNDER)
ANNOUNCER:	Your son has a priceless, God-given gift — but he may never learn to use it properly. Satisfy your child's budding curiosity by exposing him to Cartell's newest educational doll — MERV THE PERV. And MERV will return the compliment. Turn on MERV and watch your child's face light up.
ACTION:	MERV THE PERV BIT (SCREAM AND SOB)
ANNOUNCER:	MERV THE PERV — available at finer toy stores everywhere. Batteries not included.
VOICES:	SINGING ENDS — "Ding dang dong — ding dang dong"
ANNOUNCER:	This is KWKW-T-TV, Channel One, Cretin Oak, Vermont. At the tone the time will be 3 PM.
RECORD CUE:	AGAINST THE STORM THEME
ANNOUNCER:	"The End of the World" — the story of love and human understanding in a town that accepts neither, but rejects both. Brought to you by New Napalm Olive — the ultimate washday purifier in the big, bright olive-drab can. Newer than clean, cleaner than bright, brighter than white...
VOICE:	Whiter than anything.
RECORD CUE:	MUSIC UP UNDER AND OUT
ANNOUNCER:	Yesterday, Mary was released from the asylum and met at the airport by Fran and Gimp, who took her to the scene of the fire in Aubrey's stolen car...
VOICES:	MUMBLE
SOUND:	RAP RAP
LAWYER:	(OFF) Don't worry about a thing, John. (ON) Your Honor. I wish to introduce at this point...

ASST DA: I object!

JUDGE: Objection sustained.

LAWYER: All right, I'll rephrase that — I wish to introduce at this time some evidence without which my client's case...

ASST DA: I object!

LAWYER: I object! Your Honor, forgive me, but I cannot continue to press my prosecution in the face of the Assistant District Attorney's constant badgering!

JUDGE: Objection overruled. The Assistant District Attorney will remove his badger from the courtroom.

SOUND: MUMBLE

LAWYER: Your Honor, the Prosecution rests.

ASST DA: And so does the Defense.

JUDGE: This court will take a 15 minute recess and nap. Milk and cookies will be served in the cafeteria.

SOUND: MUMBLE

LAWYER: (OFF) Don't worry about a thing, Mary. He hasn't got a chance.

MUSIC: RECORD

DAD (ON PHONE): Don't worry about a thing, Louise... Yes — yes — I know — I'll talk to the... Yes... I'll have him run out of town in the next edition... Well, I'm the editor, aren't I?... I'm not?

XYLOPHONE: DING DING

DAD: Well, I'll have to call you back later, Louise. There's someone at the door... Of course I love you... I love him too. Goodbye.

MARY (OFF):	Dad?
DAD:	Oh, is that you, Helen?
MARY (OFF):	No.
DAD:	Come on in. Take off your things, you must be freezing. Would you like a drink?
MARY:	I'm back from the fire.
DAD:	Did Larry win his anti-trust case?
MARY:	Yes, they hung him.
DAD:	Thank God.
MARY:	And, Daddy — I've decided to have his baby!
DAD:	Oh, Mary, I'm so happy for you. That's wonderful. When's the blessed event?
MARY:	Just as soon after the abortion as possible.
DAD:	I will not live until I see you smile again.
RECORD CUE:	THEME MUSIC IN AND UP
ANNOUNCER:	We'll be back to "The End of the World" after this message.
VOICE OVER:	Mrs. J.S. of Pine Barren, New Jersey, doesn't know our Napalm Olive camera is focused on her.
MRS:	What I mean is — look — can you believe I'm a mother of three, and that my youngest daughter is older than I am — by looking at my hands?
VOICE OVER:	So we asked Mrs. B.J. why she was willing to take the New Napalm Olive Blindfold Test.
MRS:	No, it's true. You see — my husband is a policeman

	and you wouldn't believe how dirty he gets my clothes. I mean it. It's unbelievable.
VOICE OVER:	But we believed Mrs. P.Q. and listen to her reaction.
MRS:	I worry all night, sometimes — you know, I hate to admit it — sometimes I think my kids are doing it on purpose. It's impossible to get these clothes clean!
SOUND:	WHISTLE
SGT:	Nothing's impossible, Mam.
MRS:	Who said that?
SGT:	Sgt. Spotless of the Dirt Patrol. Our mission — to keep America clean. And when the job gets this dirty, there's only one weapon. New Napalm Olive!
MRS:	But, Sgt., look at my family — you can't get them clean.
SGT:	Negative, Mam. With New Napalm Olive, even those sneaky little yellow stains just melt away. Stand back!
SOUND:	FLAMES
MRS:	That's marvelous. All that dirt gone — and my family, too. Wait until I tell my mother.
MUSIC:	HARMONICA CHORD TRANSITION OUT
ANNOUNCER:	This is KWKW-T-TV, Channel One, Oceanside, New Mexico — Gateway to the Pacific. And now — back to "Ozzie Knows Father".

TAPED LAUGHTER

OZZIE:	Oh, gosh, Neal — what am I going to do? Help me. Don't just stand there. You're a talking horse. Don't you have any horse sense?

TAPED LAUGH

NEAL: You made the bed. You'd better lie down.

TAPED LAUGH

OZZIE: But Uncle Henry'll be here any minute, and I just can't let him see me like this.

TAPED LAUGH

NEAL: Who's looking?

TAPED LAUGH AND APPLAUSE

SOUND: KNOCK KNOCK

TAPED OOHS AND AAHS

OZZIE: Quick, Neal. Hide in the closet!

TAPED LAUGH

NEAL: You'd better hide in the closet.

TAPED LAUGH

OZZIE: Get in! Get in! Stop fooling around!

TAPED SINGLE LAUGH

SOUND: KNOCK KNOCK — PAUSE — DOOR OPENS

HENRY: What's going on here?

OZZIE: Oh! It's you, Uncle Henry.

TAPED HUGE LAUGH

HENRY: How do you explain all this?

OZZIE: Well, you see — it's all because of — er er — I don't know.

TAPED LAUGH

HENRY: Don't horse around with me, Ozzie! Who's in that closet? Stand back! I'm getting to the bottom of this!

SOUND: HORSE WHINNY

TAPED HUGE LAUGH AND APPLAUSE

HENRY: (COUGH) That's my hat!

TAPED LAUGH

NEAL: I told you never look a gift horse in the mouth!

TAPED LAUGH AND APPLAUSE

ANNOUNCER: Tune in again tomorrow at 5:30 for another hilarious adventure of "Ozzie Knows Father".

PAT BOONE: To support our boys in the Armed Service requires more than just dollars. Talking helps too. This is Pat Boo...

SOUND: XYLOPHONE THEME

ANNOUNCER: The ABC D Goldfish Television Network presents the following program in color.

VOICE OVER: Direct from our newsroom in New York, the ABC D Goldfish Evening News, with Walter Klondike — and George Matetsky in Great Mammoth, Wales; Hugh Romney in Detroit; Leon Oswald in Johnson City; Elliot Mintz in Peking; Eric Severeid on the Moon; and a special fashion report by Myna Bird Johnson, in Cold Blood, Kansas.

KLONDIKE: Good evening. The most remarkable medical achievement of modern times has entered its fourth successful day. Here with a report from Lone Star, Massachusetts, is ABC D Goldfish correspondent Felix Paparazzi.

FELIX: Here at General Hershey General Hospital, America's first man-made baby, "Tiny Tim", is developing far beyond the expectations of Surrogate General Klein and his medical staff. Doctor General, sir, how is Tiny Tim progressing?

GENERAL: We are quite frankly astonished at the rate of progression in the development of Genesis 13, since initial DMZ implantation three — er — four days ago.

FELIX: I realize that antiseptic security precautions must be maintained, but when will we be able to actually see Tiny Tim?

GENERAL: Surely not before his growth rate stabilizes.

FELIX: How many inches is he now?

GENERAL: As of an hour ago — 73.

FELIX: How is his health?

GENERAL: Excellent. He has a full head of hair, his features are normal in every respect — and pleasing, too, I might add. Our only concern now is with a certain pigmentation imbalance which has manifested in the last few hours.

FELIX: Is that serious, Doctor General?

GENERAL: No, not serious — it's a matter of personal taste.

FELIX: Thank you very much, Doctor General Klein. This is Felix Paparazzi at General Hershey General Hospital in Lone Star, Massachusetts.

KLONDIKE: Tiny Tim's incipient negritude will come as a pleasant surprise to his Honorary National Parents — Ralph Bunche and Ida Lupino... At his Press Conference today, War President Johnson answered Congressional critics of his embargo on imported goods from rebel-held Vermont with a firm "no"... The jury is still out in the Kennedy Assassination trial in Federal District court in New Orleans. Former Louisiana Governor Garrison reiterated his confidence in the outcome... An Air Lemuria DC-6 with 87 passengers aboard crash-landed safely today on the Pacific Coast Highway, while attempting an emergency landing at Walker Air Force Base, Omaha.

SOUND: PLATES AND GLASSES

JOYCE: Whew! They've all gone. Madge, will you help me put the chicken a la king back in the fridge?

MADGE: Honestly, Joyce — I don't know where you get the energy. 14 children, president of the World Bank — and you still find time to make the best buffet in Fresno. I can remember when the least little problem put you right to sleep.

JOYCE: Not anymore, Madge. Not since I discovered a simple little pill called METHEDRINE.

ANNOUNCER: METHEDRINE, available without a prescription at drug centers everywhere. Remember — METHEDRINE carries the Seal of Approval of the Armenian Medical Association.

SOUND: XYLOPHONE RIFF

SINGING VOICES: Channel One — Wonderland — in Happening Pittsville...

ANNOUNCER: KWKW-T-TV — serving Pittsville, Oildale and all of West Texas.

RECORD CUE: LOVE THEME FROM SPARTACUS

BOB: Hello, friends, and welcome to the Wonderful World of travel and adventure — THE GOLDEN HIND. Come with us as we visit strange places and people the wide world over.

RECORD CUE: MUSIC FAST OUT

BOB: Hi, friends. I'm Bob Hind. Today I'd like you to meet two of my dearest friends — George and Ida Matetsky.

GEO:	Good evening.
IDA:	Hello there.
BOB:	Well, George — you're just back from a really wonderful trip to — where was it?
GEO:	To New Guinea, Bob.
BOB:	That's right. To New Guinea. And I understand that you and your lovely wife have brought back some beautiful color films for us to see here.
GEO:	That's right.
BOB:	And we're gonna let you tell us all about it, but first let's get them on the screen here.
RECORD CUE:	MUSIC SHARP ON
BOB:	What are those, Ida? Are those natives?
IDA:	Yes, Bob — this is on the Orinoco River — probably the largest river in the vicini...
BOB:	Ah! And those are those towers you were telling me about, aren't they, George?
GEO:	Yes they are. They're centuries old.
BOB:	Oh, that one looks a little different. What is that?
GEO:	Yes, Bob. That one doesn't have a bottom.
IDA:	Oh, George — will you ever forget those romantic clam fishermen?
BOB:	Why some of those clams are as big as your hand!
GEO:	Yes, Bob — that one on the left almost nipped off Ida's hand.
BOB:	That was a close one. We'll be back to part two of THE

GOLDEN HIND.

RECORD CUE: MUSIC UP, OFF

ANNOUNCER: Gunderson's Furniture at 14019 McKissick, three blocks west of the airport at Old Oildale Highway, announces the greatest bargain bonanza in our 17 year history. Our giant Rodeo Days Sale is now going on. Just look at this — 14 rooms of factory-fresh Greek Provincial furniture — a full 12-piece bedroom set, only $89.50. And remember, with every Futura Dinette Ensemble you buy this weekend, Tom Gunderson would like you to have either this nationally advertised all-Formica toaster, or this beautiful 21 by 42 inch, completely framed, oil on velvet picture called "The Crying Clowns", by Bernard of Hollywood. Remember, that's Gunderson's Furniture, 14019 McKissick, three blocks west of the airport at Old Oildale Highway.

RECORD CUE: MUSIC SHARP OUT

ANNOUNCER: This is KWKW-T-TV, New Frisco, Nebraska. Be sure and watch at 10 tonight, as Rev. Morgan Dybbuk uncovers a threat to the life of the President on "The Possessed!"

SOUND: XYLOPHONE THEME

ANNOUNCER: The ABC D Goldfish Television Network presents the following program in color.

SOUND: BIRDS AND HORSES

HUNK: (OFF) Highpockets! Highpockets! Consarn it! Where are ya? Highpockets!

HIGH: I'm over here by the grave. Consarn it, stop shoutin', Hunk.

HUNK: Whatcha doin' out here by yerself, boy?

HIGH: Jest mopin' around, Hunk. Dad won't let me go next door an' watch the alfalfa.

HUNK:	Criminalities, boy! That wanderlust of yern is gonna be the end of us!
SOUND:	BIRDS
BRONCO:	(OFF) Hiya, Hunk!
HUNK:	Get off my back, Bronco! I'm warnin' ya — stop ridin' me!
HIGH:	Hey, leave him alone, Bronco! We's jest talkin'.
BRONCO:	I didn't mean nothin' by it. Jest foolin'.
HIGH:	Where ya bin, Bronco?
BRONCO:	Inta town. Picked up the mail — and the new schoolmarm.
HIGH:	I'll killya, Bronco! I swear I'll kill ya!
HUNK:	Hey, leave the kid alone, Bronco! You know how he feels about her.
BRONCO:	Criminentlies, Hunk! Man cain't have no fun aroun' here.
HIGH:	I'll killya, Bronco! I swear I will!
HUNK:	Hush now, boys. Here comes Pop.
SOUND:	HORSE
JEHOVA:	Howdy, boys.
BOYS:	Hello, sir — Hi Pa — Howdy Dad.
JEHOVA:	I wantcha to come away from the grave, wash your hands and faces, and get on down to the house lickity-split. Your pappy's got a surprise for ya, boy! I wantcha to come and meet your new mother. The schoolmarm.
MUSICAL VOCAL:	Bumpity-bumpity-bumpity-bump GARBANZA!

Bumpity-bumpity-bumpity-bumpity-bumpity-
Bump-bump-bump!
(REPEAT UNDER)

ANNOUNCER: GARBANZA! Brought to you by the makers of...

VOICE OVER: Loco Coco!

SINGING COMMERCIAL: Things go better with Loco Coco!
Things go better with Coke! (SNIFF)

ANNOUNCER: And by...

VOICE OVER: Anti-Chrysler Motors, makers of...

VOICE TWO: THE AVENGER. By day, a snappy pick-up. (CLICK) In the afternoon, a family convertible. (BEEP BEEP) By night — a deadly weapon. (OW!) THE AVENGER!

SINGING COMMERCIAL: See the U.S.A., through your turret-bay! Your Anti-Chrysler car will hold them off!

ANNOUNCER: This is KWKW-T-TV, McCracken Georgia. Stay tuned for the Roller Derby semi-finals at the Olymp...

CLICK!

ANNOUNCER: And now — Heeeeeere's JOHNNIE! But first...

CLICK!

SOUND: HIGH BEEP-BEEP (UNDER)

LES: ...I snapped at you, Dr. Carter — but I've had my eye glued to this telescope for three solid days.

GIRL: Les, I've never seen you so upset about a planetoid before.

LES: But the entire worl...

CLICK!

JOYCE: ...Madge. Not since I discovered a simple little pill called METHE...

CLICK!

SOUND: APPLAUSE

JEWISH COMIC: For instance, take my wife, Joey — please. But my mother-in...

CLICK!

WHITE NOISE

CLICK!

SOUND: MUMBLE

HERCULES: Osiris! Osiris! What news from Rome?

VESPASIAN: Horrible, Hercules, horrible!

HERCULES: How did you find my sister?

VESPASIAN: Raped and hanged.

HERCULES: How did you find my father?

VESPASIAN: Stoned!

HERCULES: Legions of Poseidon! On to Ro...

CLICK!

VOICE: ...okes longer, longer, longer, smoother, smoother, smoother. (TOKES) Fantast...

CLICK!

SWINE: ...let's get back to this Christ Consciousness routine, Yogi.

YOGA: No, Mr. Swine — not Christ Consciousness. Krishna Consciousness. Krishna. The Lotus Feet of...

SWINE: All right, all right, sit tight Swami — or whatever you call your...

CLICK!

SOUND: KNOCK KNOCK

BOY: Two minutes! Two minutes, Miss Lamont!

VERA: I can't go on, Sol. I can't go on! (CRYING)

SOL: Now, wait a minute, Vera. You gotta go on. Those boys out there have fought their way all the way from Anzio to hear you sing. Just remember one thing — if it weren't for them, the President of the United States would be named Schickelgruber.

RALPH: Hiya, friends. Ralph Spoilsport, owner and operator of Ralph Spoilsport Motors here in the city of Downer. And here's Tony Gomez to talk to our friends below the border –

TONY: Hola, amigos Latinos. Aqui a Ralph's Used Motors, mil trescientos North Hoover a la esquina de 42nd Place, tenemos millares de automoviles superiores y barratos. Por ejemplo — aqui es un carro magnifico — un 1949 Hudson Hornet, equipado con todos los power extras.

SOUND: CAR NOISES

TONY: Aqui a Ralphs, el precio completo solamente doscientos sesenta-seis dollars. Doscientos sesenta'seis dollars. Al contado, veinte-ocho dollars con approved bank credit. Aqui, un otro bargain fantastico. Por la familia con muchos niños, un '38 Dodge Pickup. Precio todo, ciento dollars. Usted puedo usar su Bankamericard, Ralph's Credit Plan o cash. Y ahora back to the movie.

M.C.: And here she is, boys! Uncle Sam's answer to the Japs — Miss Vera Lamont!

SOUND: WHISTLES AND APPLAUSE

VERA (SINGS): When the lights come on again, all over the world,
And our boys come home again, all over the world.
Come on boys!

BOYS (SING): You had a good home, but you left.
(OFF) You're right!
You had a good girl, but you left.
(OFF) You're right!
Sound off! (OFF) One two!
Sound off! (OFF) Three four!
Cadence count! One two...

ANNOUNCER: We interrupt the Late Late Show to bring you this bulletin from the KWKW-T-TV newsroom. This late word from New Orleans. The jury has returned a verdict in the Kennedy assassination trial. Former Louisiana Governor James Garrison has been found guilty on all counts. His attorneys will appeal the decision directly to the War President's Spiritual Advisor. And now — back to Channel One's The Late Late Show — Babes in Khaki.

BOYS (SING): We'll fight, and kill!

VERA (SINGS): You bet you will!

BOYS (SING): For nothing can stop the Army Air Corps!

SOUND: END TITLE MUSIC UP AND OUT

ANNOUNCER: This is KWKW-T-TV, in Gourd of Ashes, Wyoming. And now, we conclude our broadcast day with BY BREAD ALONE — a message of faith and inspiration, delivered this morning by his Eminence, Father O'Long of the First Jansenist Church.

RECORD CUE: AGAINST THE STORM

FATHER: Dear Lord. We thank you for sustaining us through another day. May the power and the glory of thy word guide us through dark and troubled waters, and help us to comprehend the incomprehensible, even though we can never understand it. Amen.

VOICES: HUM "FROM SEA TO SHINING SEA"
SING (FALSETTO): Oh beautiful, for spacious...

CLICK!

WHITE NOISE

CLICK!

WHITE NOISE

CLICK!

TONE

CLICK!

WHITE NOISE

CLICK!

SOUND: PLANES (OVER)

SOLO TENOR: Oh say does that star-spangled banner yet wave,
O'er the land of the free, and the home of the brave?

WHITE NOISE

RECORD CUE: BEATLES "A DAY IN THE LIFE"

So long, Uncle Pete.

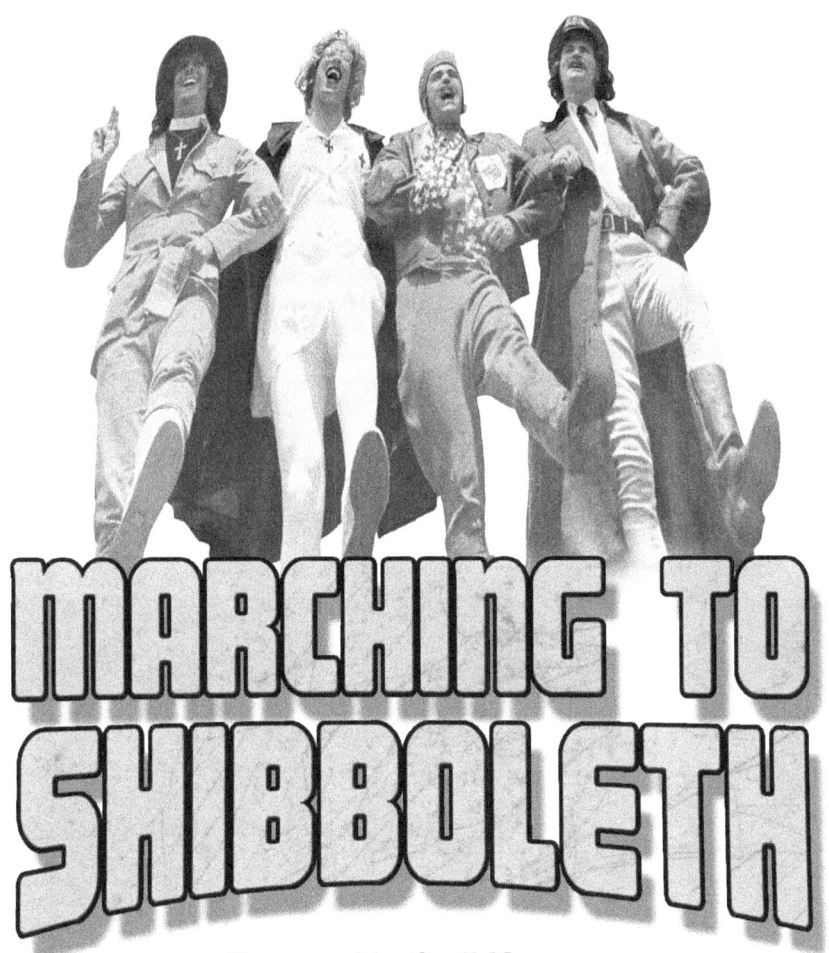